THE H

MW00576105

CHRISTOPHER CLAPHAM

The Horn of Africa

State Formation and Decay

HURST & COMPANY, LONDON

First published in the United Kingdom in 2017 by
C. Hurst & Co. (Publishers) Ltd.,
41 Great Russell Street, London, WC1B 3PL
© Christopher Clapham, 2017
All rights reserved.
Printed in India

The right of Christopher Clapham to be identified as the author
of this publication is asserted by him in accordance with the
Designs and Patents Act, 1988.

A Cataloguing-in-Publication data record for this book
is available from the British Library.

ISBN: 9781849048286

This book is printed using paper from registered sustainable
and managed sources.

www.hurstpublishers.com

CONTENTS

CONTENTS

ACKNOWLEDGEMENTS

This book is the product of an interest in the Horn of Africa stretching back over many years, and my first and greatest debt is to all those—and especially those Eritreans, Ethiopians and Somalis—who have done their best to help me gain some understanding of the region over the years. It is a complex, fascinating and frequently exasperating part of the world, almost every aspect of which is subject to controversy and contestation. All I can claim here is that I have attempted to provide an overview of the developments of the last quarter century that I hope that some readers will find enlightening, even though others will doubtless find much with which they disagree. That is in the nature of the subject, and I have felt it more useful to attempt to impose a single and relatively coherent picture of the region's recent experience, even at the cost of simplification, rather than try to take account of widely varying and often contradictory views in a way that would inevitably become confusing.

One great compensation of studying the Horn is that the region's historical depth, its social complexity, and the traumas through which it has passed in recent years have attracted the attention of a community of scholars, both indigenous and external, whose fascination with the area is every bit as great as my own, and on whose research and insights I have been able to

ACKNOWLEDGEMENTS

draw. The brief bibliography at the end of this book lists only those works that I have directly cited, and necessarily omits (since such a list would probably be longer than the book itself) a vast amount of material that has helped to inform and shape my understanding, often no doubt in ways of which I am unaware. However great the differences between them, scholars of the Horn are deeply aware both of the peculiar pull of the region itself, and of belonging to a tradition of enquiry stretching back to the great Hiob Ludolph in the later seventeenth century, from many of whose modern representatives I have learnt more than I can say. I owe a particular debt to a number of colleagues who have read parts or all of this book in draft, and saved me from some at least of the errors into which I would otherwise have fallen. These notably include Gaim Kibreab, Goitom Gabreluel, Ken Menkhaus, David Styan, Kjetil Tronvoll, Sarah Vaughan, Harry Verhoeven and Michael Woldemariam, as well as two very helpful but anonymous publishers' readers. It is more than usually necessary to emphasise that none of these share any responsibility for any of the views that I have expressed.

I have in addition two institutional debts. The first is to the Centre of African Studies at the University of Cambridge, which has provided me with a welcoming home in my retirement (or at least semi-retirement), and with a stimulating environment encompassing the whole of the African continent and a great variety of disciplinary perspectives. The second is to the Rift Valley Institute, whose annual residential courses on the Horn, taking place in different countries in eastern Africa, provide a wonderful opportunity for scholars, aid workers, diplomats and other practitioners in the region to meet and learn from one another. It has been in response both to the need for me to articulate my own views on the subject, and to the amount that I have learned from other participants, that I have developed many of the ideas expressed in this book; and I hope that they

ACKNOWLEDGEMENTS

will be of some use, not only to fellow academics, but to those who seek to put their understanding of the region to use in ways that will (I trust) benefit its peoples.

Christopher Clapham

Centre of African Studies,
University of Cambridge
September 2016

LIST OF ACRONYMS AND INDIGENOUS WORDS

ADLI	Agricultural Development Led Industrialisation (Ethiopia)
al-Itihaad al-Islamiya	Somali Islamist movement
al-Shabaab	'the Youth': Somali Islamist movement
AMISOM	African Union Mission in Somalia
ANDM	Amhara National Democratic Movement (Ethiopia)
AU	African Union
Birr	Ethiopian currency unit
CJTF-HOA	Combined Joint Task Force—Horn of Africa (US military)
CPI	Transparency International, Corruption Perceptions Index
CUD	Coalition for Unity and Democracy (Ethiopia)
Derg	Provisional Military Administrative Council (Ethiopia, 1974–1991)
EEBC	Eritrea-Ethiopia Boundary Commission
EECC	Eritrea-Ethiopia Claims Commission
EFFORT	Endowment Fund for the Rehabilitation of Tigray (Ethiopia)
ELF	Eritrean Liberation Front

LIST OF ACRONYMS AND INDIGENOUS WORDS

EPDM	Ethiopian People's Democratic Movement
EPLF	Eritrean People's Liberation Front
EPRDF	Ethiopian Peoples' Revolutionary Democratic Front
EPRP	Ethiopian People's Revolutionary Party
ESDL	Ethiopian Somali Democratic League
FDRE	Federal Democratic Republic of Ethiopia
FGS	Federal Government of Somalia
FRUD	Front for the Restoration of Unity and Democracy (Djibouti)
G-15	Group of Fifteen (Eritrea)
Gabar	Peasant (Ethiopia)
GERD	Grand Ethiopian Renaissance Dam
Gim gima	Internal discussion and self-criticism within the TPLF
Guurti	Somali traditional assembly
ICU	Islamic Courts Union (Somalia)
IGAD	Intergovernmental Authority on Development
Kebelle	Urban Dwellers' and Peasants' Associations (Ethiopia)
LAPSSET	Lamu Port, South Sudan and Ethiopia Transport Corridor
Meison	All Ethiopia Socialist Movement
Metek	Metals and Engineering Corporation (Ethiopia)
Nakfa	Eritrean currency (and town in northern Eritrea)
Neftenya	Armed settler (Ethiopia)
OAU	Organisation of African Unity
OLF	Oromo Liberation Front (Ethiopia)
ONC	Oromo National Congress (Ethiopia)
ONLF	Ogaden National Liberation Front (Ethiopia/Somalia)
OPEC	Organisation of Petroleum Exporting Countries
OPDO	Oromo People's Democratic Organisation

LIST OF ACRONYMS AND INDIGENOUS WORDS

PFDJ	People's Front for Democracy and Justice (Eritrea)
Salafism	A 'fundamentalist' form of Islam, emphasising return to the purity of the original faith
SEPDM	Southern Ethiopian Peoples' Democratic Movement (Ethiopia)
SNM	Somali National Movement (Somaliland)
SNNPRS	Southern Nations, Nationalities and Peoples' Regional State (Ethiopia)
SNP	Somali National Party (Somaliland)
SPLA/M	Sudan People's Liberation Army/Movement (South Sudan)
SPM	Somali Patriotic Movement
SRRC	Somalia Reconciliation and Restoration Council
SRSP	Somali Revolutionary Socialist Party
SSDF	Somali Salvation Democratic Front
Tegadelti	Liberation war fighters (Eritrea)
TFG	Transitional Federal Government (Somalia)
TNG	Transitional National Government (Somalia)
TPLF	Tigray People's Liberation Front (Ethiopia)
UEDF	Union of Ethiopian Democratic Forces
UNMEE	United Nations Mission in Ethiopia and Eritrea
USC	United Somali Congress
Xeer	Somali customary law
WSLF	Western Somali Liberation Front (Ethiopia/Somalia)
WYDC	Warsai-Yikaalo Development Campaign (Eritrea)
Zoba	Region (Eritrea)

Map 1: The Horn—Altitude, with State Boundaries

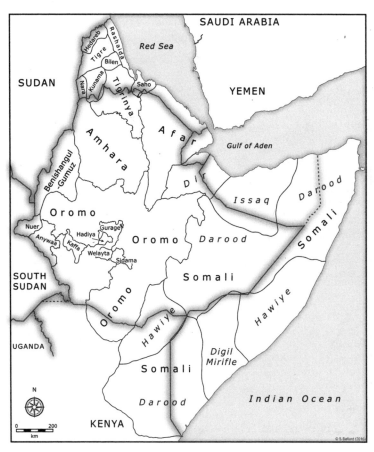

Map 2: The Horn—Major Population Groups

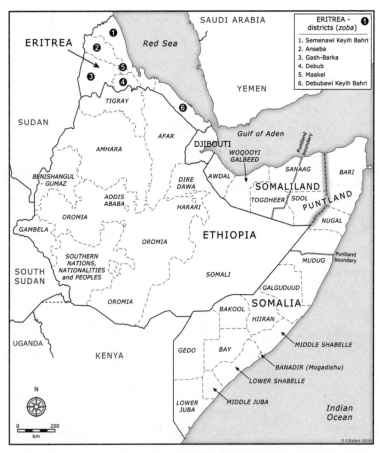

Map 3: The Horn—Administrative Subdivisions

INTRODUCTION

AN AFRICAN ANOMALY

The Horn of Africa, so named from that great wedge of north-eastern Africa that projects like a bull's horn into the Indian Ocean, consistently figures as the part of the African continent that does not fit into those generalisations—themselves often stereotyped and simplistic—through which the continent is frequently described. To the outside world, it has appeared as a region not merely anomalous but deeply problematic. In the mid-1980s, it came most dramatically to global attention through the Ethiopian famine, and the pitiful spectacle of people dying in very large numbers, simply because they did not have enough to eat. This human catastrophe, and the relief effort that it prompted in the Western world, imprinted a picture of the region as a disaster zone that has not entirely faded even three decades later. In the early 1990s, it was Somalia that captured the headlines, through the complete collapse of the basic structure of order—the state—on which humanity's capacity to manage the planet, and to assure the provision of necessities to its people, has come to rely. This led to a massive intervention by the United States—'doing God's work' as the then US President George H.W. Bush put it—that was entirely unable to rectify, and may even indeed have exacerbated, the failures that had

1

prompted it. More broadly, this is a region historically characterised by appallingly high levels of conflict, which has taken the
form both of guerrilla warfare, and of 'conventional' wars
between states, to a degree unequalled in other parts of Africa.
The long Eritrean struggle for the independence that it eventually gained in 1991 achieved an epic status in the history of
insurgent warfare; and in Eritrea and Somaliland, along with
immediately adjacent South Sudan, the Horn provides the only
cases in Africa in which secessionist movements have succeeded
in winning the independence of particular regions from the states
into which they were previously incorporated.

This book is centrally concerned with the dynamics of state
formation and decay in this peculiar part of Africa. It first seeks
to explore the distinctive origins of states in the region, in terms
of its physical environment and its history, and then examines
the very different trajectories of the region's states—different
both from one another, and from much of the rest of Africa—
since the critical year, 1991, in which its inherited state structures collapsed, and attempts to construct new states in their
place began. It is the central argument of the book that the
dynamics of the Horn are essentially home grown. This is despite
the fact that the region has been deeply affected by external
influences since the very earliest times, attested by the establishment of both Christianity and Islam from only a relatively short
while after their creation in adjoining parts of what we now
describe as the Middle East, and possibly also of Judaism. Much
more recently, the Horn has also provided the most striking
incursion into Africa of the global rivalries of the Cold War. But
in all these cases, external powers both spiritual and military have
been absorbed into the existing structures of the region, and have
contributed to conflict (and in some cases also to peace) in ways
that owe more to their configuration to local circumstances than
to anything inherent in those powers themselves. Reduced to

brutal simplification, the Horn may be described as constituting *non-colonial* Africa, as contrasted with the states of the rest of the continent south of the Sahara that may be conceived essentially, despite the enormous differences between them, as the successors to European colonialism. The central political feature of the Horn has been the survival at the core of the region of the only indigenous sub-Saharan African state, the Ethiopian empire, to retain its independence through the era of colonial conquest. As the area under the control of the Ethiopian empire expanded or contracted over many centuries, virtually all the peoples of the region came at one time or another under its sway. In the colonial era, indeed, this empire not only survived but massively expanded its own territory, emerging as by far the region's largest state by population, and imposing its presence on its neighbours. This in turn explains why even those parts of the Horn that were colonised—Italian Eritrea, the French Somali Coast (now Djibouti), the British Somaliland Protectorate, and Italian Somalia—were subordinated to non-colonial dynamics to a degree that did not occur elsewhere.

It is this distinctive experience that drives the definition of the Horn used in this book, as comprising Ethiopia, Eritrea, and the Somali territories that came under Italian, British and French colonial rule. Some studies of what has been termed the 'greater Horn' have extended the region to include both Kenya and the Sudan (with now independent South Sudan), and even as far afield as Rwanda. It goes without saying that no region however defined can be completely separated from its neighbours, and in this case the relationship with Sudan has been particularly important. The Sudanese state nonetheless owes its existence (and its own distinctive problems) to its relationship to Egypt and the Nile, rather than to that with Ethiopia and other territories to its east. Kenya has been drawn into the Horn especially by the very large ethnically Somali population in the northeast part of its territory, but nonetheless exists essentially as the successor to the former British colony, and its dynamics are driven internally by the relationships between the peoples of its most densely inhabited central zones, and regionally by its historical connections to the other former East African colonies of Uganda and Tanganyika (now Tanzania), rather than by those with the states to its north and east. Each of these states will be brought into the narrative where relevant, but this book is not basically about them.

Scholars concerned with different themes have understandably adopted different definitions that reflect the questions that they are seeking to answer. Alex de Waal's superb recent study of the tactics of political survival in the region, for example, draws heavily on the cases of Sudan and South Sudan, which illuminate the issues with which he is concerned, while finding only a marginal place for Ethiopia, where politics operates in rather different ways.[1] Any study of regional security would be likely to spread the net still more widely, in acknowledgement of the presence in Somalia of military forces not only from Kenya, but from Uganda and even Burundi. A growing concern for the regional politics of Islam has undermined the conventional distinction between 'sub-Saharan Africa' on the one hand, and the 'Middle East' on the other, and started to resurrect ancient linkages across the Red Sea and the Gulf of Aden. It is not just because of the Horn that the United States' only military base in Africa, Camp Lemonnier, is situated in Djibouti. Definitions, in short, are mere framing devices, driven by the needs that they are intended to serve.

This book's quest for the distinctiveness of state formation in the Horn drives us into deeply historical questions about why the states of the region exist, and how they have come to take the peculiar forms in which we now find them. A certain amount of basic history is correspondingly unavoidable, and forms an essential backdrop to any attempt to understand the peculiarities of the region. Its primary concern, however, is with developments since 1991, the climactic year in which the overthrow of the incumbent regimes in both Ethiopia and Somalia, and the subsequent dismemberment of both states with the emergence of independent Eritrea and quasi-independent Somaliland, vividly demonstrated the failure of existing political structures virtually throughout the region, and laid bare the need to construct new political orders on the ruins of the old. Coming as it did at a moment when the end of the Cold War, the collapse of *apartheid* in South Africa, the evident bankruptcy of many existing postcolonial African regimes, and popular pressures for essentially Western-style multi-party democracy throughout Africa were prompting similar agendas for renewal in the rest of the continent, this might well have been expected to lead to some convergence between post-colonial Africa and the hitherto distinctive countries of the Horn. In fact, this did not happen, and the Horn continued on its deviant course, with consequences that continue to shape the peculiarities of the region, and—given not least that the earlier periods have been extensively covered in existing works, whereas the more recent developments have been subject to only patchy scrutiny—make the current era one of particular interest.

The peculiar status of the Horn as what I have termed 'noncolonial Africa' raises in turn that great counter-factual of African history: how might the continent have developed, had it not been for the nineteenth-century colonial partition? This is, to be sure, a very open question. Other parts of Africa would certainly have followed distinctive paths, determined by the specific features of their own internal dynamics. But insofar as the Horn has anything to offer, its answers are not particularly reassuring ones. The most remarkable difference is that the frontiers between the states of colonial Africa, ludicrously imposed and artificial though these were, have survived intact through more than half a century of independent statehood, and nowhere appear to be seriously contested, whereas the frontiers of the Horn are far more contentious. Indeed, it may plausibly be argued that it was the very artificiality of the territories of formerly colonial Africa, imposed from afar in ways that had virtually nothing to do with the identities of their own indigenous peoples, that allowed the leaders of the states of independent post-colonial Africa to agree to leave their boundaries intact, in the form in which they were inherited from an alien colonialism. Territories created by internal sources of power, whether in the form of Ethiopian conquest or Somali nationalism, were far more problematic, since these sources of power remained vivid and contested in ways that a now defunct colonialism did not, with potentially very divisive consequences. In terms at least of the relations between independent African states, the impact of colonialism on Africa appears—by reference to the counter-example of the Horn—to have been paradoxically stabilising. In other ways, however, legacies of statehood dating back to long before the colonial era, or culturally established mechanisms for conflict management, may offer countervailing strengths to states and societies that continue to conceive themselves in non-colonial terms.

But if the Horn is to be distinguished by its 'non-colonial' status, that in turn raises the question of *why* this part of Africa should have been able, as it were, to 'escape' the impact of colonialism on the rest of the continent. The answers to that question are to be found especially in the geophysical structure of the region, which in turn was to have a massive, and in some degree indeed determining, impact on its societies and history. This is where the quest for an explanation has to start.

1

THE POWER OF LANDSCAPE

Introduction

In a world on which human beings appear to have imposed their control, to an extent that has led the present era to be called the 'anthropocene', it is salutary to be reminded that human societies have been created by the physical geographies to which they have been required to adapt or die, and that in some parts of the world these geographies continue to impose themselves to a striking degree. There can be few regions for which this is more evidently the case than the Horn of Africa, and any attempt to account for the distinctiveness of the Horn must therefore start from a simple picture of what it looks like.

It is a region characterised, most of all, by dramatic *differences* in land forms, immediately adjacent to one another, which in turn have therefore led to the evolution of different modes of livelihood, and thus to different kinds of society, different social structures and values, and correspondingly different forms and perceptions of political power. At the most basic level, the high incidence of conflict that has occurred within the region can be explained by the ways in which such discrete societies have been brought into direct and often brutal contact with one another.

Not for nothing is this one of the most seismologically active zones on the face of the planet, where in the Afar Depression inland from the Red Sea coast, straddling the present frontier between Eritrea and Ethiopia, seething bubbles of molten lava are forcing their way to the surface, and are likely to lead in the fullness of geological time to the separation of the areas south and east of the Great Rift Valley that cuts through the centre of the region from those to the north and west.[1] The most dramatic effect of such activity in the distant past has been to create a highland zone unequalled anywhere in Africa, the Ethiopian Plateau. Generally situated at some 2,000 metres in altitude, though rising at its highest point, Ras Dashen in Ethiopia, to just over 4,500 metres, this has been high and therefore cool enough, and has attracted sufficient rainfall, to permit settled cultivation. At the same time, it has been present for long enough for deep ravines to be formed that carry this rainfall to the surrounding lowlands, greatest among them the gorge of the Abbay or Blue Nile, which provides by far the greater part of the water that has for millennia sustained the civilisations of Egypt, some 2,500 kilometres to the north.

The interface between highland and lowland is at its sharpest where the eastern edge of the highlands drops into the Rift Valley, most spectacularly between Asmara and Massawa in Eritrea. To the west and north, the change in altitude is not so dramatic, but still sharp enough for the mountains to startle any passenger looking out of the window of an aircraft approaching from Egypt or Sudan. The lowlands to the north, east and south of the central massif are for the most part a country of thorn scrub and very limited rainfall, suited only to animal pastoralism, save for the possibility of irrigated or flood recession agriculture along the watercourses that drain the highlands. A third zone, and one of increasing importance in recent times, occupies broadly the south-western quadrant of Ethiopia, and is high enough in altitude and rich enough in rainfall to support tropical forest, albeit generally degraded as the result of long human occupation, and to provide crops of which the most familiar to the outside world is coffee, which grows wild in the region of Kaffa, after which (at least according to Ethiopian lore) it is named.

John Markakis[2] has usefully described these three zones as the 'highland core', the 'lowland periphery', and the 'highland periphery' respectively, and even though he applies these terms only to Ethiopia, the distinctions that they express are common to the whole region, and provide a convenient way to characterise the varying societies of the Horn. These very terms ascribe a privileged position to the 'core', which has provided an understandable source of grievance to the peoples of the other areas, whom it implicitly degrades to a lowlier status. Whatever sympathies this arouses, there is nonetheless a logic to it. Not only are the highlands, and especially the northern plateau, the geomorphological feature that most clearly distinguishes the Horn from other parts of Africa, but they have historically created the power structures to which the peoples of the peripheries have been, and to a large extent continue to be, subordinated, and to which, therefore, they have to react. If you want to understand this region, this is where you have to start. The element of discrimination that unquestionably exists is built into the structure of the Horn, not merely derived from the prejudices of this or any other author.

The Highland Core

The area often described as 'historic Ethiopia', or sometimes as 'Abyssinia' (from the name commonly used in Europe until 1936, and used in the form 'Habasha' in the country itself), broadly follows the contours of the northern highland zone from north of Asmara in today's Eritrea to the Ethiopian capital,

Addis Ababa. Defined by the edge of the Rift Valley to the east, and less sharply to the west, it is broadly commensurate with the territory occupied by the Tigrinya-speaking peoples in highland Eritrea and the Tigray region of northern Ethiopia, and the Amhara further south, though conquest and population movement have inevitably blurred the boundaries, especially to the south and west. Though Addis Ababa, for example, now falls squarely within the territory of the Oromo (of whom much more later), the ruins of an ancient monolithic rock church on the Entoto hills in the north of the city show it to have been in medieval times part of the Christian empire.

It is a zone defined technologically by ox-plough agriculture, the only such area in the whole of sub-Saharan Africa. However primitive this may appear, with the single tine of the plough little more than scratching the surface of the soil, it nonetheless made possible a level of arable farming that placed northern Ethiopia on a level broadly comparable to medieval Europe, and similarly permitted a relatively dense population. This was critical. It gave *land* a centrality not only to the survival but to the mentalities of its peoples that has survived to the present day, and is expressed in conceptions of territoriality without which the vicious and extremely damaging 1998–2000 war between Eritrea and Ethiopia—the two inheritor states of the northern highland culture—over trivial areas in dispute on their common frontier would be virtually incomprehensible. And provided that too close a comparison with medieval Europe is not built into the term, it created societies that may generically be described as 'feudal'. As in Europe, it made possible the extraction of a surplus that led to the emergence of a ruling group who not only benefitted from the toils of a subordinate peasantry, but were also able to impose the forms of control that arable agriculture required.

Hierarchy, rather than collaboration between equals, is thus the guiding principle of highland society. As one Amhara peasant commented to the anthropologist René Lefort at the time of the 2005 Ethiopian elections, 'we are a people to be governed'.[3] This capacity for government and the level of organisation that goes with it underlies the extraordinary durability of the states that have been erected on it, the ancestry of which can be traced to the kingdoms of Yeha and Axum before the onset of the Christian era. Allied to Orthodox Christianity, which came to the region as early as the third century, it underlay the creation in the twelfth and thirteenth centuries of the rock-hewn churches of Lalibela, one of the wonders of the world. In the late nineteenth century, it was the critical factor in explaining how Ethiopia, alone among the states of pre-colonial Africa, retained its independence through the period of colonial conquest. A century later, it enabled the peoples of Eritrea and northern Ethiopia to sustain guerrilla insurgencies of a resilience unequalled in Africa, and only very rarely found elsewhere. It is the rock on which the distinctive experience of this part of Africa—including the elements of conquest, brutality and exploitation that are likewise very much part of its legacy—has been founded.

It is nonetheless a structure not without its problems, and is in some ways deeply flawed. The demands of obedience on which it is built are instrumental—founded on calculation—rather than unconditional. An Amhara proverb, 'you bow in front—and fart behind',[4] perfectly reveals that combination of apparently obsequious deference coupled with a subversive sense however concealed that underlies its attitude to authority. Power is respected from below, only insofar as it can be shown to be effective from above. Any deviation from subordination is correspondingly akin to rebellion, and the scope for expressing disagreement with a leader while at the same time respecting his authority are characteristically extremely limited. It lends itself to a level of secrecy and intrigue that differs sharply from the ideals of openness and

11

accountability that underlie the principles of liberal democracy. It is likewise expressed through a mania for control on the part of those in authority that makes it very difficult to tolerate the levels of autonomy needed, for example, to sustain a modern capitalist economy. The continued state control of telecoms in both Eritrea and Ethiopia, which leads to communications markedly more expensive and less efficient than in, say, Kenya (or even Somalia), or the difficulties experienced by foreign businessmen under the constant and intrusive interference of state officials, are the result every bit as much of deep-seated cultural legacies as of specific government policies.

As the triumph of the Eritrean People's Liberation Front and the Tigray People's Liberation Front in 1991 likewise indicates, habits of obedience can be used to challenge central authority as well as to sustain it. The deep physical fissures that separate different parts of the northern highland plateau from one another have historically helped to sustain regional identities, and made it possible for great provincial lords to build local power structures that owed only nominal obedience, if that, to the emperor who stood at the apex of the pyramid of power. Over much of the history of ancient Ethiopia, there was no fixed capital, because the emperor was engaged in constant movement throughout his territory, in order to protect its frontiers and keep his vassals under control. During the hundred years between the mid-eighteenth and mid-nineteenth centuries, a period known as the 'era of the princes' or *zemena mesafent*, central government in Ethiopia was displaced by regional warlords, who fought one another for supremacy. It was the Ethiopian state's good fortune that in the period immediately prior to the European scramble for Africa, a succession of extremely capable emperors was able to restore the power of the central authority enough to enable it to present effective resistance to its invaders. Exactly the same process may well be regarded as much less fortunate for those neighbouring peoples who found themselves conquered and ruthlessly incorporated into an Ethiopian state that was every bit as expansive in its ambitions as the European colonial empire-builders, and rather less inhibited by the principles of modern 'governance' that, even in the age of empire, to some extent constrained its European competitors.

All ethnicities, nonetheless, are to some extent fluid, and this fluidity is encouraged in the societies of the northern highlands by the principle of bilateral descent. Whereas in most African cultures, to which lineage is characteristically extremely important, descent is traced primarily either through the male (patrilineal) or female (matrilineal) line, in this region each enjoyed a broadly equal status, and hereditary rights in land in particular could be claimed either through one's father or one's mother. This made it relatively easy to blur one's identity, by selectively emphasising the most advantageous line. Both grandfathers of the last Ethiopian emperor, Haile Sellassie, to take a particularly striking example, were Oromo, and his maternal grandmother is generally believed to have been Gurage, a small group from the area southwest of Addis Ababa. It was his descent through his father's mother from the royal family of Shoa, northeast of Addis Ababa, that provided his genealogical claim to the throne, and he was universally regarded as an Amhara. It has in turn been relatively easy for anyone to 'become' Amhara, by adopting an Amharic name, speaking the Amharic language, accepting Orthodox Christianity, and generally behaving as though one was Amhara, a process that has eased the gradual formation of a sense of Ethiopian nationhood. A similar process may be underway with the association of Tigrinya-speakers with the state in Eritrea. Among Somalis, who trace their ancestry overwhelmingly through the male line, and for whom genealogy is something of a cultural obsession, such fluidity would not be possible. This is therefore the point at which to examine what the distinctive experience of the Horn has looked like from the very different perspective of its 'peripheral' inhabitants.

The Lowland Periphery

Surrounding the highlands on every side, the peoples of the lowland periphery stand in the most striking contrast to those who have just been discussed. They belong to a great variety of self-identifying and linguistic groups, from the Nara and Kunama of western Eritrea to the Rashaida and Afar of the Red Sea coast, the Somali—by far the largest and most important of the lowland peoples—who occupy a vast territory from Djibouti through Somaliland, Somalia and southeastern Ethiopia to northern Kenya, the Boran Oromo of the Kenya-Ethiopia frontier zone, and the Anywaa, Nuer, Beni Shangul and Gumuz along the borders between Ethiopia and South Sudan and Sudan. Differentiated in many ways, they also have much in common, particularly significant being pastoralism as a way of life. Few parts of this vast area are suited to settled agriculture, the major exceptions being Lake Assaita where the Awash river sinks into the Afar depression, the highlands east of Harer in Ethiopia that extend into Somaliland, and the Wabi Shabele and Juba river valleys in south-western Somalia. Animal husbandry as a way of life—with camels as the dominant beast in the Red Sea plains and the Somali zone, cattle in the south and southwest—imposes critical constraints on those who practise it. Population densities are necessarily low, save for the key watering places where the herds and flocks are compelled to gather during the driest periods in what are normally severely water-short areas.

The social and political structures of the pastoralist zone derive from these conditions. Conflict is inherent in societies in which people and animals are engaged in competition over desperately meagre resources, with dry season water as the resource most critical to survival. The boundaries so vital in allocating the liveli-hoods of settled agriculturalists are meaningless at best, deeply offensive at worst, among peoples who are constantly on the move. Territorial identities are irrelevant to those who have no fixed territories, and *states*—the form of territoriality that has come to define governance in the modern global system—are extremely difficult to create and maintain among pastoralist peoples, and have characteristically been imposed on pastoralists by people (whether indigenous to the region like the northern highlanders, or alien to it like European colonialists) who seek to control the areas in which they live. Among all the pastoralist peoples of the Horn, only the Afar have historically possessed a political system with some affinity to statehood, the Aussa sultan-ate, which derived from its control of the lower Awash river and Lake Assaita, which provided a permanent source of water and thus of power, and contrasted dramatically with the aridity of the rest of their territory. The Afar, however, were divided by colonial rule between Ethiopia, Eritrea and the French territory now known as Djibouti, and the sultanate has faded from the scene.

Pastoralists therefore encounter states primarily as an alien form of domination, and evade or resist them when they can, or else use them in an entirely instrumental way to benefit from different jurisdictions on either side. Boundaries in the pastoral-ist zone are difficult to define, and practically impossible to police. Highlanders constantly seek to impose themselves on lowlanders, whom they despise as mere nomads with no fixed abode. As an Amhara proverb has it, 'he who has no home on earth will have none in heaven'. Only very rarely does a combina-tion of highland disorder and charismatic lowland leadership lead to characteristically devastating pastoralist incursions into the highlands. The most traumatic such incident in the history of the northern highlands, the *jihad* of Imam Ahmad ibn Ibrahim al-Ghazi, known to Ethiopians as Ahmed Gragn (the left-handed), remains embedded in the Ethiopian consciousness five hundred years after it occurred.

In the absence of states, pastoralists must organise themselves socially in very different ways, most important among which is lineage or descent. Friends and allies are essential in the struggle for resources, and your own kinsfolk are the most reliable place to find them. The 'clan', a group defined by descent from a common male ancestor, is thus the classic social formation of the lowlands. Rigid in its definition, save that individuals may be able to attach themselves to it by an invented or symbolic genealogy, it is extremely flexible territorially. In a world of extensive population movement, to which pastoralists are particularly receptive, fellow clansmen in the Gulf or the United States retain their links and their obligations to those in their region of origin, obligations expressed for example in remittances that are vital to the welfare of relatives caught in the vicissitudes of drought or warfare back home. Linkages of hierarchy are correspondingly weak, and make it extremely difficult to build those structures—such as an army, or a bureaucracy—that are central to state-based organisation. Such means as are available to bridge the divisions between groups defined by descent depend on conventions of negotiation between equals, rather than on subjection to a common power. These are indeed essential, though the settlements that they devise are generally limited and difficult to enforce.

One key source of the common values needed to pre-empt or resolve conflict is religion, and specifically Sunni Islam, which defines the social values of the pastoralist periphery in the same way that Orthodox Christianity does in the northern highlands. Of all the pastoralist peoples of the Horn, only those of the south-western lowlands of Ethiopia adjoining South Sudan are not Moslem. The cultural, political and economic divide between the zones is thus also a religious one—and one in which, like the Christianity of the highlands, Islam reaches back to the earliest years of the faith. The peoples of the coastline just across the Red Sea from the origins of Islam in Arabia were among the earliest converts to the new religion. The graveyard of a long-abandoned settlement on the island of Dahlac Kebir, off Massawa in today's Eritrea, bears tombstones with Arabic inscriptions dating back to the second century of the Muslim era. The self-identification of Ethiopia as a Christian island in a Muslim sea is thus of very long duration. Historically, the Islam of the Horn has been of an undemanding character, largely taken for granted by its adherents and readily accommodating the customs of the different peoples whom it encompassed. Few women were veiled, and pilgrimages to the tombs of revered holy men, notable among them Sheikh Hussein in the Bale region of southern Ethiopia, and the founders of the major Somali clans, have been among its most prominent manifestations. The recent growth of more puritanical and literalist versions of the faith, characterised as Salafism, has therefore marked an important change in the social and political impact of Islam.

The political character of the region's religious frontier has varied markedly according to the historical processes by which it was formed. Along the sharp eastern edge of the northern highlands, interaction between the two religions is of very long standing, and a mutually acceptable *modus vivendi* has generally been reached. Ethiopian tradition records that the Prophet's earliest followers took refugee there from persecution in Arabia, and that he ordered them in gratitude to respect the faith and independence of the Ethiopians. The highland-lowland frontier was an essential source of trade between the produce of the two regions: the salt bars known as *amolé* that were used as currency in the highlands came up on camelback from the Afar depression. The Muslims also controlled the Christians' access to the sea, essential not only for trade, but to retain the Orthodox Church's links to its co-religionists in Coptic Egypt, which until the twentieth century supplied the Ethiopian patriarch.

In other areas, the relationship was altogether more conflictual. In the centre of the ancient Muslim walled city of Harer, captured by the Ethiopians in the 1880s, is a large Orthodox Church, imposed as a brutal symbol of conquest. Beside it stands an equestrian statue of the victorious Ethiopian general, Ras Makonnen, father of the future emperor Haile Sellassie. In Jigjiga, now capital of Ethiopia's Somali region, a statue of their own hero Imam Ahmad ibn Ibrahim, conqueror of Christian Ethiopia, has recently been erected. In parts of the southern highlands of Arsi and Bale, inhabited by Muslim Oromos, the relationship is marked not only by conquest, but by the allocation of their land to the conquerors, who reduced its previous owners to the status of a servile class exploited by Christian landlords. The alienation created by such treatment runs very deep. In Eritrea, whose population is divided almost equally between the adherents of the two religions, the complex relationship, examined later, has been shaped by the legacies of liberation war.

By far the most numerous and important of the pastoralist peoples are the Somali, who are also exceptional in that in very few other parts of the world do pastoralists provide the leaders and indeed entire populations of states, rather than suffering the normal fate of pastoralists and being incorporated, with greater or lesser levels of force, into states controlled by settled peoples. Somalis therefore provide the one lowland people whom it is essential to examine in greater detail. They are in many ways a remarkably homogeneous group. They share a myth of descent from a common ancestor, Somal, a common language, a common religion in Sunni Islam, and a pronounced sense of common identity. Despite the presence of some historic cultivators, notably in the Wabe Shabele and Juba valleys, they also share a culture very heavily derived from the demands of pastoralism. Far more than most peoples in the Horn, or indeed the whole of Africa, they may be characterised as a 'nation'.

Turning them into a nation of a politically usable kind has been a very different matter. For a start, Somali culture is marked by a powerful egalitarianism, in which—in marked contrast to the northern highlands—relations of hierarchy and deference are minimal, and political authority is correspondingly hard to maintain. As one nineteenth-century English traveller was told, for Somalis 'every man is his own sultan'.

Such authority as is recognised derives mostly from attributes personal to the individual: piety, wisdom, or the embodiment of some wider cause. In few societies are poets so revered, for their ability to put into memorable words ideas or opinions that are widely shared. To this must be added the impact not simply of 'clan', but of fissures that arise at every level, and that are, as already noted, inherent in the character of pastoralist societies.

At the highest level, these distinguish what are often described as 'clan families', which group together a number of clans that share a common descent. Among these the Darood are generally regarded as the largest, and are spread especially across the northeastern and central zones of the Somali territory; the term 'Ogaden', often applied to the whole of Somali-inhabited Ethiopia, is actually the name of the Darood clan most prominent in the area. Their pre-eminence is contested by the Hawiye, whose political weight is greatly increased by their control of the capital city, Mogadishu. A third clan family, the Isaaq, are heavily concentrated in the north central part of the Somali territories that was to become the British Somaliland Protectorate, and have correspondingly been associated with political regionalism, in contrast to the other major groupings, including the Dir, whose dispersal across a wide area disposes them to more pan-Somali political projects. A final grouping, the Rahanweyn or Digil-Mirifle, have been concentrated in the river valleys of southern Somalia, many of them living as cultivators rather than pastoralists, and correspondingly despised by members of clans who view themselves as representing a purer form of Somali culture. As a weak group inhabiting a rich area, they have been particularly badly affected by the constant conflicts in southern Somalia in recent years.

Though each clan is broadly associated with a 'home' territory, the boundaries of such territories are constantly contested, as a result both of the demands of life on the hoof, which creates regular migrations that bring clans into contact and therefore conflict with one another, and of the emergence of sources of wealth that instantly attract claims from rival clans that seek to control them. The port city of Kismayu in southern Somalia has become a focus for such conflict in recent years, as the centre for the profitable charcoal trade—which has also resulted in the further degradation of an already fragile ecosystem. But clan conflicts and solidarities do not arise only at the level of the clan family or the individual clan, but at that of the sub-clan or sub-sub-clan, or whatever level is appropriate to the resources that are being fought over.

A life of constant conflict in a harsh environment rapidly becomes unsustainable, and though Somalis are certainly capable of sustaining conflicts which (to outsiders, at least) appear to be mutually destructive, survival also calls for mechanisms for their management or resolution. To some extent, this can be handled through generally accepted customary law (or *xeer*), though it says much for the underlying level of violence that this extends to appropriate compensation for homicide. 'Elders', whose status characteristically derives from recognition of their personal character rather than simply age, are in frequent demand for managing disputes. Women, who for the most part have a deeply subordinate status, may gain an ability to mediate between their own patrilineal clan and that of their husband, inter-clan marriage being an accepted way of linking different clans. Large scale conflicts may be resolved through a grand gathering of all those involved, known as a *guurti*, which hammers out a settlement over days or weeks of endless argument and compromise. And occasionally, some common cause may bring everyone together under a charismatic leader, albeit invariably only for a limited period, until this unity breaks down into familiar quarrels and rivalries. These mechanisms have come under increasing pressure as a result of the traumas which Somalis have suffered in recent years. *Xeer*, for example, provides mechanisms for dealing with low-level disputes, and is remarkably effective in helping to sustain the remittance system on which many Somalis now depend, but is ill-equipped to manage large-scale communal violence, and additional forms of conflict management are certainly needed to cope with the problems of modern Somali governance.

What a society constructed in this way appears to lack is a capacity for long term systemic change or 'development'. The same patterns are endlessly replicated. In some ways, Somalis are admirably suited to the demands of the modern world, notably through migration that extends the nomadic existence to a global level, and that enables them to build resilient long distance trading networks that do much to mitigate the impact on individuals of at best unsettled conditions in their region of origin. They instantly appreciated the value of the mobile telephone as a means of maintaining social linkages over long distances. Somali neighbourhoods have sprouted not only in Nairobi and Addis Ababa, but in Minneapolis. But all these mechanisms represent ways of extending values and patterns of behaviour generated in the pastoralist environment into previously unfamiliar settings. They do not indicate much change in those values and patterns of behaviour themselves, least of all the ability to build the institutional mechanisms needed to establish stable and peaceful modes of existence within their own homelands. Though as we will see, some means of managing Somali societies have proved in recent years to be far more effective than others, the pastoralist ethos remains deeply antipathetic to the demands of peace, human welfare and good governance that lie at the heart of the developmental project.

The Highland Periphery

This discussion has left until last the group of peoples most critical to the future of the Horn: those who, living in regions (that is to say, at altitudes) that permit settled agriculture, and accustomed to the basic levels of governance that settlement requires, have at the same time been largely excluded from the existing structure of states. Living overwhelmingly in central, southern and western Ethiopia, though represented also by the Bilen and Tigre peoples of western highland Eritrea, they have as a result of the later nineteenth-century partition become largely involuntary subjects of states which derive in one way or another from the highland core. The capacity of this part of Africa to move beyond the historical legacies of conflict, to create generally stable political systems geared to the welfare of their peoples, depends on whether they can be incorporated as full citizens into their states, on an equal and voluntary basis,. The pastoralists by contrast have little option but to adapt themselves to whatever settlements are or are not made in regions at higher altitude.

The most important of these groups, and indeed the largest ethnic group in the Horn (and possibly the largest in Africa), are the Oromo, who are almost entirely resident in what is now Ethiopia, with just a small number in Kenya. Their current territory stretches north from the Kenya border to central Ethiopia, almost as far east as Harer, and then westwards through the Addis Ababa region nearly to the frontier with Sudan and South Sudan, as well as up the escarpment to eastern Welo and southern Tigray. Originating in the Kenya-Ethiopia borderlands, they expanded rapidly from the sixteenth century through one of those great population movements that punctuate the history of Africa, overrunning in the process parts of the Ethiopian empire and the territories of anyone else who stood in their way.

In their homelands, they practised a remarkable constitutional system known as *gada,* in contrast both to the hierarchies of the northern highlands, or the regulated anarchy of the Somali, in which each age grade—those born over a given eight-year period—succeeded its predecessors in specific governmental functions. Surges of Oromo expansion can be correlated with the point at which a new warrior grade took over, impelled to surpass the exploits of its predecessors. This system broke down under the pressures of expansion, and as they took over new lands, they adapted to the demands of the environment in a way that dramatically illustrates how the societies of the Horn have been shaped by local modes of livelihood. In the north, where they encroached on the northern highlands, they became almost indistinguishable from Amhara, though many of those who spread up the escarpment into Welo adopted Islam rather than Christianity. These became deeply integrated into the politics of the Christian empire from the later seventeenth century onwards, and for substantial periods effectively controlled the imperial government. It was from this group that emperor Haile Sellassie derived his Oromo ancestry. Where they abutted onto Somali territory in the east, Kereyu Oromo became camel herders like their neighbours. In much of western Ethiopia, they formed small kingdoms of their own, notable among them the Jimma sultanate deep in the forest zone.

In religious terms likewise, the Oromo reflected the diversity of their regional environments. Those in what is now eastern Ethiopia, from the Arsi and Bale highlands north to Welo, became Muslim, as was the sultanate of Jimma in the southwest. In central northern Shoa, they were Orthodox Christian, while those, especially in the west, who retained indigenous systems of

23

belief until the modern era, were open to proselytisation by European missionaries, many of them from Scandinavia, and became Protestant Christians. Of the two main Protestant denominations in Ethiopia, *Mekane Yesus* is Lutheran in origin and largely of Scandinavian derivation, while *Kale Heywet* is Calvinist and draws on the converts of the Sudan Interior Mission which spread into southern Ethiopia from southern Sudan. These, along with other groups, spearheaded the rapid expansion in Evangelical Christianity that has been a striking feature of religion in Ethiopia as in other parts of Africa in recent years, and has drawn converts from the Orthodox Church.[5]

In short, the Oromo form a microcosm of the peoples of Ethiopia, and as the largest single 'nationality' in the country, and also the most centrally placed and occupying much of the most economically developed part of the country, they might well have been expected to take a very prominent—even dominant—political role, using their diversity to integrate many at least of Ethiopia's other groups. Had Ethiopia followed what was to become the normal trajectory of the rest of sub-Saharan Africa, with over half a century of colonial rule followed by the formation of a nationalist movement and a period of open political competition leading to independence, it is more than likely that this would indeed have happened. Instead, the place of the Oromo in the political configuration of Ethiopia has been obstructed in two main ways. First and most obviously, the political construction of the country has been imposed to a very large extent by the peoples of the northern highlands, and derives from the historical legacies of the Orthodox Christian empire. This was the organisation that created the modern Ethiopian state in the later nineteenth century, and continued to dominate it thereafter. The 'national' language of the country, or effectively the language of government and thus of education, was Amharic rather than Oromifa. Northern highland dress and food came to be presented and perceived as 'national' traditions. Peoples from other groups, many Oromo among them, effectively 'became Ethiopian' by becoming Amhara, or at any rate Amharised. Second, the very diversity of the Oromo made it extremely difficult to create any common identity or organisation through which the idea of Oromoness could be expressed. A sharply increased sense of 'being Oromo' has become apparent in recent years, but a *usable* sense of what this actually involves has been much harder to devise, not least against the pressures presented by the counter-identity of an essentially Amharised Ethiopianness. This is now emerging as the core cleavage in the creation of a stable and effective national polity, perhaps outranking even that between Christianity (in its now diverse forms) and Islam. The problems of the highland periphery in Eritrea are in some ways comparable, though there the demographic advantage lies with the Tigrinya-speaking highland core.

But the Oromo are very far from being the sole representatives of the 'highland periphery' in Ethiopia. The most densely inhabited parts of the country, which lie in its fertile and for the most part highland southwest quadrant, are neither Oromo nor Amhara, and under the present constitutional order are grouped together in the cumbersomely entitled 'Southern Nations, Nationalities and Peoples' Regional State', or SNNPR. These include a large number of different groups, most populous among them the Sidama, Welayta, Kambatta and Gurage. Their livelihoods are assured not by the grain cultivation of the northern highlands or the pastoralism of the lowland periphery, but by a great variety of indigenous crops, most important and distinctive of which is *enset* or false banana, a striking plant that resembles the banana, but the food source of which is provided by the roots. Its cultivation permits very high population densities, and it is also far more resistant to drought than either grain or animal husbandry. The downside is that it tastes disgusting.

The 'southern peoples' were subject to exactly the same processes of northern highland conquest and subordination as the Oromo, with levels of variation (as also occurred between different groups of Oromo) according to whether they resisted conquest or accommodated themselves to it. They are more likely to have adopted the *Kale Heywet* or Calvinist form of Protestant Christianity, whereas the Lutheran or *Mekane Yesus* form is more closely associated with the Oromo. Their incorporation into the state was less problematic than that of the Oromo, not least because as relatively small groups of no more than a few millions, they were in no position to articulate an identity that could challenge that of the Amhara at the national level. In addition, the area of *enset* cultivation was far less attractive to northern landlords and colonisers than the grain-producing terrain of the Oromo, with the result than northern domination was generally less brutally exploitative at the local and personal level. Some of the southern peoples, notably the Gurage, emerged as the most commercial and entrepreneurial of Ethiopia's inhabitants, and thereby gained interests in a national identity and the growth of towns, most obviously Addis Ababa.

The Population Dynamics of the Horn

Even before the great partition of the late nineteenth century, the peoples of the Horn, like those of the rest of sub-Saharan Africa, were linked in all manner of ways: through population movement, acculturation, religion, long distance trade, and adaptation to environmental stress, as well as through conquest and resistance. Reasonably accurate maps of the region were published in Europe from the late seventeenth century onwards, much earlier than for most of the African interior, and the knowledge that these displayed reflected not only contacts with Europe, but also the interactions between indigenous peoples.

These were not isolated societies locked away until the onset of modernity in the guise of colonialism.

This had its familiar effects, notably through the increased levels of movement and interaction that resulted from the imposition of common systems of rule, and especially the establishment of cities that attracted individuals from throughout the newly created territories. Only for Ethiopia is any census information available, and in 2007 Addis Ababa included individuals who identified themselves as belonging to seventy-five distinct Ethiopian ethnic groups, dominated by Amhara (46.1%), Oromo (19.5%), and Gurage (16.3%).[6] Even so, the distinctive experiences of the Horn have affected the region's populations in specific ways, most evidently in Ethiopia, where the role of an Amhara-dominated central government has been reflected in the spread throughout the country of individuals who identified themselves as 'Amhara' (though many of these may well have originated from other groups, and come to see themselves as Amhara, as noted above), either through government or as the result of settlement. The region's experience of conflict has also given rise to widespread processes of 'ethnic cleansing', notably the flight or expulsion of highland settlers from other parts of Ethiopia as the result of the 1974 revolution or the post-1991 introduction of ethnically-based federalism, and of Somalis back to their original clan homelands after 1991. Many Ethiopians left Eritrea after independence in 1991, while the outbreak of war between Ethiopia and Eritrea in 1998 resulted in the expulsion of Eritreans from Ethiopia.

A further effect of conflict has been the creation of large diaspora populations, who continue to have a significant impact on the politics of their homelands. Somalis have been especially mobile, and the earliest Somali settlers in the United Kingdom, for example, were nineteenth-century seamen. By 2014, there were an estimated 114,000 Somali-born residents in the UK, with a total population of Somali origin (including those born in the UK, or immigrating from third countries) probably in excess of 150,000.[7] There were probably a similar number in the United States.[8] The preference of Somalis to concentrate in specific areas (including Eastleigh in Nairobi and Bole in Addis Ababa, as well as Minneapolis in the United States) has both restricted integration into their host societies, and promoted their continued relationships with their country of origin, most evidently through the remittances on which many Somalis throughout the region continue to rely. Many expatriate Somalis retain dual citizenship, and become deeply engaged in domestic Somali politics. A very high proportion of the leading members of the Somali Federal Government, to take a striking example, are US passport holders. Eritreans have likewise fled their homeland in large numbers, as a result both of the war for independence between 1965 and 1991, and of the military conscription which, as noted in Chapter Four, has turned the country into one of the largest producers of refugees in the world. Ethiopian emigration to the United States reached significant numbers with refugees from the revolutionary regime after 1974, and Americans of Ethiopian origin probably number about half a million.[9] Many members of all these groups are intensely engaged in the politics of their countries of origin, and—enjoying a freedom of expression through the electronic media that is often denied to their compatriots back home—foster impassioned debates that represent a much wider range of opinions than is available locally. As a result, the politics of the Horn has now become thoroughly transnationalised.

Although the broad outlines of the region's population dynamics are clear enough, there is a marked lack of reliable statistical information. Only Ethiopia has conducted any recent national census, and for other countries in the region even such basic data as total populations and growth rates are unavailable. Nor is there any information on such critical issues as the breakdown of the Somali population by clan affiliation, or the numbers of each of the ethnic groups within Eritrea. Much of this information is in any event politically sensitive, and national authorities (where they exist) may well have an interest in suppressing it. The widely repeated assertion that Eritrea, for instance, is roughly equally divided between Christians and Muslims, is no more than an assumption, and were accurate figures to become available, these might then be used to challenge (or conversely to reinforce) a political structure in which power is disproportionately wielded by Christian highlanders. The levels of displacement resulting from conflict and bad government add a further element of uncertainty. The available estimates nonetheless make clear the massive predominance of Ethiopia, which with roughly ten times the population of Somalia (including Somaliland), twenty times that of Eritrea, and a hundred times that of Djibouti, accounts for over 85% of the region's people.

Table 1: Population Estimates by Country, 2016

Djibouti	Eritrea	Ethiopia	Somalia/ Somaliland
893,780	5,281,340	100,658,562	10,904,271

Note: These figures are estimates for 1 January 2016, from http://countrymeters.info/en/. They are highly speculative, as only Ethiopia has had a census in recent years. An official estimate for Eritrea, which is likely to overestimate rather than underestimate the total population, is 3.2 million in 2010, or only 60% of the figure given here,[10] and reinforces the very low reliability of estimates such as this. The figures for Somalia include Somaliland, which is estimated (https://en.wikipedia.org/wiki/Somaliland) to have a population of about 4,000,000. There are no available figures for the breakdown of population between ethnic groups within Djibouti and Eritrea, or between clans within Somalia.

A further critical issue is population growth, for which the countries of the Horn share demographic features characteristic of sub-Saharan Africa as a whole. As with other figures, those for population growth are often little more than guesswork, but those for Ethiopia show an increase in total population from 18.4m in 1950 to 35.4m in 1980, and 82.9m in 2010.[11] Projections, which are of course highly speculative, run to 145m by 2050, according to United Nations demographic estimates, whereas the Worldometers website projects 188.5m by the same date,[12] a discrepancy that indicates the extreme caution with which such figures should be treated. Both the rate of population growth, and the pressure that this places on living standards, depend heavily on government responses, notably with regard to health services and other social policies, agricultural productivity, and general economic growth, but provide an insistent backdrop to the politics of the Horn.

2

HISTORIES OF STATE CREATION
AND COLLAPSE

Structures of Partition

The great late nineteenth-century carve-up of Africa that laid
down the territorial grid that eventually resulted in today's structure of African states likewise took place in the Horn, but—
characteristically—did so in a way significantly different from
that in the rest of the continent, and left behind it a pattern of
state formation that differed not only in the internal character of
the resulting political units, but in the dynamics of relations
between them. Central to this was the survival at the core of the
region of Ethiopia, the sole indigenous sub-Saharan state to
defeat its would-be colonial conquerors and emerge into the
twentieth century as an independent country. The critical
moment, the battle of Adwa in the Tigray region of northern
Ethiopia on 1 March 1896, when the Ethiopian army under
emperor Menilek II decisively defeated the invading Italian
forces, was certainly a close-run thing. At a time of famine
prompted by the great rinderpest epidemic that swept through
eastern Africa in the 1890s, the Ethiopian forces were on the

31

point of falling apart from lack of food when the battle occurred. The Ethiopians were likewise fortunate that one of the strongest of African states found itself up against one of the weakest of European colonial ones, the newly united kingdom of Italy. At the core of the Ethiopian achievement was nonetheless the ability of Menilek's government to put together an army of over 100,000 men, most of them armed with modern rifles, on the distant northern frontier of the country at a time of severe economic hardship. This was a feat that no other pre-colonial African state came even close to matching.

So far as the future of the region was concerned, it had two major consequences. The first was the formation and continued independence of the Ethiopian state itself, a state that extended well beyond the highland core that had for many centuries formed the heartland, and for much of the time indeed the sole territory, of the empire. Menilek had closely followed and shrewdly appreciated the designs of the European states, and had played them off so adroitly against one another that many of the rifles that defeated the Italians had been supplied by colonial powers who sought his support against their rivals, including by the Italians themselves. He likewise recognised that at a time of colonial conquest, he was in a position to play the same game himself. "If powers at a distance come forward to partition Africa between them", he wrote in a circular to European governments, "I do not intend to be an indifferent spectator".[1] His own home region of Shoa, at the very south of the highland core, was already expanding over the areas to the south and west, and this process rapidly accelerated in order to pre-empt European conquest. At one point, indeed, the Ethiopian armies even reached as far as the White Nile south of Khartoum, before being obliged to retreat in the face of the advancing British forces. Even so, the territory thus incorporated was vast, more than quintupling the area under Ethiopian control, and perhaps tripling or quadrupling its population.[2]

The result was to create an empire significantly different from the European empires being established in Africa at the same time. One advantage, certainly, was that the conquerors were not sharply divided from the conquered by race, as was the case elsewhere, though highlanders often retained an arrogant sense of superiority over those whom they treated as little more than slaves. Those local rulers who accepted Ethiopian overlordship were generally permitted to remain in power (as was likewise the case in the European colonies), whereas those who resisted were crushed. The sultan of Jimma in the southwest reached an accord with Menilek, under which Christian churches were excluded from his domain, whereas the neighbouring kingdom of Kaffa, which resisted, was destroyed. A measure of intermarriage took place, normally involving conversion to Christianity, and individuals from the conquered territories sometimes attained high rank in the imperial government. Nonetheless, an internal colonialism was in some ways more problematic than an external one. The colonised peoples of the European empires were all broadly equal in their subjection, despite the tendency of the colonial rulers to favour some groups over others, whereas conquest by an indigenous power carried with it a premise of inequality. English, French or Italian were neutral languages of rule, as between indigenous peoples, but Amharic very clearly privileged one of those peoples over others. And while the eventual growth of a political consciousness among the colonised could in other parts of Africa be predicated on a 'nationalism' that brought together the peoples of the colony, however artificial the unit concerned may in origin have been, such a consciousness among 'new Ethiopians' would instead be directed against the existing and unequal structures of internal rule. As happened elsewhere in Africa, 'settlers' were in some regions imposed on the local populations, inevitably arousing particularly intense hostility, but this practice was more widespread in

33

Ethiopia, where retired soldiers of the imperial army (known as *neftegna*, or man-with-a-gun) were given land in the conquered territories together with control over the peasants (or *gabar*) who farmed it, and effectively constituted a local occupying force. The tensions underlying this experience constitute a significant part of the reason why Ethiopia, alone in Africa, was subsequently to experience a genuine revolution.

The second consequence of Ethiopian independence was the fragmentary nature of the surrounding European colonies. Formed along the coasts of the Red Sea, Gulf of Aden and Indian Ocean, with the effect of cutting off Ethiopia from direct access to the sea, they were prevented from expanding into their hinterland by Ethiopia's continued existence. This was most evidently the case with the Italian colony of Eritrea. Formally established in 1890, Eritrea provided a base for the subsequent invasion of Ethiopia, though it also served as a colony for Italian settlement. The central part of the territory was inhabited by Orthodox Christian Tigrinya-speaking highlanders, who had from the earliest times formed part of the Ethiopian state. Early indigenous resistance movements against the Italian conquest were conducted in the name of continued loyalty to Ethiopia. After his victory at Adwa, however, Menilek did not seek to drive the Italians into the sea, or even to reoccupy historically Ethiopian territory. This was probably wise, given the state of his own army and the danger that incursion into an area recognised as an Italian colony might have induced retaliation not just from the Italians but from other colonial powers, though Tigrinya-speakers have sometimes seen it as a manoeuvre to divide and weaken their own part of the country, to the advantage of Menilek's homeland of Shoa.

Eritrea therefore remained an Italian colony, gaining some prestige in Italian eyes as the 'colonia primagenita' of the newly united Italian state. Effectively it served as an entry point to northern Ethiopia, for which Massawa provided access to the sea, to the extent that regional lords in Tigray would travel through Massawa and then by sea to Djibouti in order to reach Addis Ababa, rather than make the long journey by muleback overland. This gave the Italians ample opportunities to build relationships with the northern lords, with the idea in mind of renewing the attempt to conquer Ethiopia when an opportunity arose. Critically, they took no steps to demarcate on the ground the precise border between their own territory and Ethiopia, providing ample opportunity for confusions that might later create a *casus belli*. This was an omission that was later to lead to much bloodshed and hostility between Ethiopia and by then independent Eritrea.

When Mussolini came to power in Italy at the head of the Fascist regime in 1922, Eritrea became one of the focal points for a revived Italian nationalism, and a construction boom took place that has left Asmara, the capital, with some of the finest Art Deco architecture in the world. More ominously, it reinstated Eritrea's role as a launchpad for the invasion of Ethiopia that took place in 1935. By this time, developments in the military sphere had transformed the strategic balance between the two countries, including notably air power and the widespread use of illegal poison gas. Heroic Ethiopian resistance was in vain, and after an eight-month war, the Italians entered Addis Ababa in May 1936, declaring an Italian East African empire that stretched from Eritrea in the north to the Indian Ocean coast of Somalia in the south, the only period of recorded history in which Ethiopian independence has been extinguished.

But if military developments worked in favour of Italy, global political and diplomatic ones conversely favoured Ethiopia. The future emperor Haile Sellassie, who had (as Ras Tafari) become regent and head of government in 1916 before gaining the throne in 1930, sought to boost Ethiopia's international standing by joining the League of Nations in 1923; and although the League cruelly disappointed his hopes that it would provide its promised protection against aggression in 1935, this did at least establish Ethiopia's status as an independent state, with the result that when the Italians were defeated after engaging in the second world war on the side of Nazi Germany, Ethiopia regained its independence under a restored emperor. Its status as a victim of fascism, and a timely alliance with the United States, also enabled it to persuade the United Nations to approve the federation of Eritrea with Ethiopia in 1952, an outcome fraught with very damaging consequences. Ethiopia's outstanding diplomatic skills can be traced to the long period, from Menilek onwards, during which diplomacy has been central to the state's survival.

While the Italians occupied the Red Sea coastline, the French established themselves in the Gulf of Tajura at the southern end of the Red Sea, creating the French Somali Coast with its capital at Djibouti. This proved a much less contentious initiative, since the French did not seek to colonise Ethiopia, but instead contented themselves with building a port that would serve the central and southern parts of the country, constructing a railway from the coast that reached Addis Ababa in 1916. This has, ever since, been a role that has suited both partners very well, and has enabled Djibouti, tiny enclave though it is, to survive through the intervening period as the only territory in a very troubled part of the world that has remained largely at peace.

Whereas colonialism in Eritrea and Djibouti (which in addition to Somalia had a substantial Afar population) had the normal effect of bringing disparate peoples together under alien rule, its impact on the greater part of the Somali-inhabited Horn was precisely the opposite: it divided Somalis between different jurisdictions—no fewer than five of them. As well as Djibouti, these comprised the British Somaliland Protectorate along the Gulf of Aden coastline (a colony initially created to guarantee a supply of meat to the garrison in Aden), Italian Somalia facing the Indian Ocean, a substantial area of British Kenya, and not least the large central zone taken over by Ethiopia. Of these, British Somaliland was governed with a nonchalance appropriate to its marginal status: British interests in Ethiopia were concerned largely with the control of the Nile waters, an issue of critical importance to Sudan and Egypt, both of which at that time were under effective British control. British colonial relations with Ethiopia in both Kenya and Somaliland were limited to managing the fractious activities of pastoralists along their common frontiers. And although Italian Somalia formed the southern part of the projected (and briefly realised) Italian East Africa, it was separated from Ethiopia by a large zone of inhospitable scrub, and had nothing like the importance of Eritrea. In the disposal of former Italian colonies by the United Nations after the Second World War, it was handed back to Italy under the guise of a UN trust administration. The frontier between Somalia and Ethiopia has, formally at least, never even been defined, let alone demarcated: the line that appears on maps, and has been tacitly accepted by both sides, is no more than the provisional administrative boundary unilaterally established by the temporary British military administration in 1941.

The impact of colonialism on the Somalis also meant that the peoples of these territories (like Eritrea, but for different reasons) did not follow the standard pattern elsewhere in Africa of forming territorial nationalist movements that sought and eventually gained independence within the existing colonial boundaries. Instead, Somali nationalists sought independence for a single united Somali state that would bring all Somalis together under a common jurisdiction. This was in essence the project that had led to the creation of a united Italy and Germany in the mid-nineteenth century, and in a European context it would have been unproblematic. In the context of a postcolonial Africa, in

37

which fragile and newly independent states have been defined by a rigid adherence to the existing colonial frontiers, it was deeply subversive. It directly threatened not only Ethiopia but also Kenya, and by extension challenged the territorial legitimacy of virtually every state on the continent. Once again, the peculiar patterns of state formation in the Horn set the region apart from the rest of Africa.

In the longer term, the legacies that this process of partition imposed on the Horn were to prove disastrous, and led to wars both civil and external, to appalling levels of bloodshed and destruction, and to the failure of the states throughout the region that were charged with the attempt to manage them. The remainder of this chapter will examine this failure, with reference to Ethiopia and Eritrea on the one hand, and to the Somali territories on the other.

Empire, Revolution and State Failure in Ethiopia and Eritrea

On returning to power with the defeat of the Italian invaders in May 1941, the restored emperor Haile Sellassie set about creating an effective, centralised and modernising state, many of the elements of which remain in place to this day. He was, within the limitations of his own upbringing and the situation within which he was placed, an extraordinarily skilful ruler, adept at managing both a complex domestic political situation and the changed world within which Ethiopia had to operate. His first priority was to reduce his dependence on the British, who had (alongside a valiant contribution by the Ethiopian resistance) defeated the Italians, and at that time also ruled virtually all of Ethiopia's neighbours, including most critically Eritrea, which became an 'occupied enemy territory' under British administration. This he achieved by building a close relationship with the United States, which survived until the end of his reign.

Though American aid contributed to establishing much of the institutional base of the restored empire, its most significant immediate dividend was in Eritrea, where US diplomatic muscle was critical in securing the vote in the UN General Assembly for a federation between Eritrea and Ethiopia, "under the sovereignty of the Ethiopian crown". A lively politics over the territory's future had emerged under the British, which mobilised the identities of its different religious and ethnic groups, and resulted in no very clear consensus. The Ethiopian government heavily backed the 'unionist' cause, which favoured 'reunion' with Ethiopia, and was especially strong among Tigrinya-speaking Orthodox Christian highlanders with long historic links to the Ethiopian state, though even there some misgivings were expressed. Other groups opted for separate independence, or for a partition that would assign the Moslems of the western lowlands to Sudan. The eventual UN resolution endowed Eritrea with an elected regional government with a substantial degree of autonomy, while leaving foreign affairs, defence and other critical functions in the hands of Addis Ababa. The most important benefit that the United States gained from the deal, apart from a regional ally in a strategically sensitive area adjoining the Middle East, was a communications base near Asmara which, in an age before satellites, provided a critical link in its global military command-and-control system.

Domestically, the centrepiece of the Ethiopian modernisation project was an expanded education system, designed to create a class of technocrats to staff the institutions that it would require. The brightest secondary school pupils were sent abroad for university education, while a university college was established in 1951, and greatly expanded after 1960. These provided competent and at times outstanding management skills, and created an elite, many of whom were assigned to agencies set up to handle technical tasks outside the normal government ministries. One of the most prominent of these, Ethiopian Air Lines, remains in recognisable form today, and others included the Imperial Highway Authority, the National Bank of Ethiopia, the Awash Valley Authority (the precursor of numerous 'virgin lands' development schemes under subsequent regimes), and many more.

One striking triumph was that the imperial government was able to place itself diplomatically at the head of the emerging group of independent African states, hosting the conference in May 1963 that led to the formation of the Organisation of African Unity, with emperor Haile Sellassie as its first chairman, and with Addis Ababa as its permanent headquarters. That a regime so strikingly unlike any of its African equivalents should have been able to establish such a position of leadership was a tribute to the diplomatic skills involved. Indeed, Ethiopia was able to benefit from the fact that it was *not* one of the newly independent post-colonial states. Standing apart from both Francophone and Anglophone Africa, straddling the gap between Arab north Africa and sub-Saharan Africa, avoiding premature commitment to any of the competing groupings of African states set up immediately after independence, Ethiopia could also draw on the prestige of an emperor with his own anti-colonial credentials in the struggle against Italian fascism, with a status that distinguished him from the competition for primacy between nationalist leaders such as Nasser, Nkrumah, Nyerere, Sekou Touré or Senghor. It was an achievement with a lasting impact, that was to turn Addis Ababa into the diplomatic capital of Africa, and give Ethiopia an important advantage in its dealings with African rivals.

But while all this presented an encouraging impression of steady developmental progress, the political basis of the regime was fatally flawed. A 'revised constitution' promulgated in 1955 established a lower house of parliament elected by universal suffrage (though the senate was directly appointed by the emperor), but with no political party system (and certainly none would have been permitted) this was in no position to build any grassroots political base. The regime was tightly controlled by the emperor in Addis Ababa, and ministers from the prime minister downwards, however capable as individuals, were in essence imperial technocrats. A very high proportion of them came from the Shoa region around Addis Ababa, and the peoples of the south and west, incorporated into the empire in the late nineteenth century, were virtually unrepresented. In sharp contrast to the nationalist movements in colonial Africa which were at the same time creating organised and partisan popular political structures, this failure of representation prompted a top-down political mobilisation through centrally placed elite groups and institutions, which was eventually challenged only by guerrilla warfare, and created a markedly different form of politics from that found elsewhere in the continent.

Nowhere were the regime's political failings more starkly exposed than in Eritrea, where it proved quite incapable of managing or even co-existing with the elected Eritrean government established under the terms of the UN resolution. The imperial viceroy in Asmara (who was the emperor's son-in-law) set about steadily degrading its capabilities, even though it was entirely run by unionist politicians who had supported Eritrea's 'reunification' with Ethiopia. By 1962, the central government was able to induce the Eritrean parliament, under strong pressure, to disband itself and vote for the full incorporation of Eritrea as an ordinary province of the Ethiopian empire. Officially hailed as the final step in the full reunion of Eritrea with the 'motherland', this fatally alienated many Eritreans from the unionist project, and helped to promote armed resistance to the imperial regime. Though dated by Eritrean nationalists to 1961, this resistance became evident from the mid-1960s, and provided the first of the guerrilla insurgencies that were to affect the entire region.

A further critical turning point was a *coup d'état* attempted in December 1960 by the Imperial Bodyguard, the elite corps of the armed forces, which sought to replace the emperor by his son, and institute a much more dynamic process of political change. The rhetoric of the coup leaders, who were forcibly suppressed within a few days, referred to the 'backwardness' of Ethiopia in comparison with the developments taking place elsewhere in Africa. Equally symptomatically, the plotters were supported by university students, who demonstrated in their support. From that point onwards, students were to emerge through the 1960s as the most vocal opposition to the regime, while also building links with the younger officers in the armed forces whose aspirations came to match their own.

The imperial regime was destroyed essentially as the result of its evident incapacity to handle the political challenges that a new era imposed on it. A legitimacy derived from the divine right of kings attracted little more than derision from educated Ethiopians who, far from remaining content with the technocratic status that they were assigned, developed political ideas of their own.[3] There was little place among these for Western-inspired liberal democracy, which in an Ethiopian context would have empowered the rural areas that were assumed at least to be deeply conservative in their political orientation, and radical opponents of the regime sought to seize power at the centre. From the later 1960s, the students were almost entirely committed to Marxism-Leninism, though in differing and often intensely competing forms. One major source of division was what was known, following Marxist-Leninist terminology, as the 'national question'. The pre-eminence of the emperor excluded any mechanism to provide the peoples of the empire or their representatives with any meaningful role in government, and the regime's 'nation-building' project could offer nothing more than the possibility of assimilation into the language, culture and political values of the highland core. Deep-seated problems deriving from control over land, especially in the highland periphery, could not be addressed when the landowners were entrenched in the imperial system of government that had created these problems in the first place. The war in Eritrea intensified, to which the regime could respond only by increased repression. Lower level revolts and insurgencies appeared in other parts of the empire.

The *coup de grace*, when it came, was delivered at the centre. A strike early in 1974 by taxi drivers protesting against fuel price increases deriving from the OPEC-inspired oil price rise rapidly escalated into strikes and demonstrations by virtually every organised group in the capital, students as usual well to the fore. The dismissal of the prime minister, and his replacement by a more reformist administration derived from the same group of palace-based politicians did nothing to stem the upheaval. Government indifference to a famine in the Welo region of the northern highlands helped to undermine the emperor's carefully fostered image as the benevolent father of his people. The junior ranks of the army started to play a covert but ominous role. And in September, the emperor was deposed, his standing by that time so diminished that he was merely arrested and driven off to imprisonment in the back of a Volkswagen beetle.

The reformist regime that followed, under a senior general of Eritrean origin, lasted no more than two months, before power was seized by a hitherto shadowy military grouping, the Provisional Military Administrative Council, generally known as the *Derg*. This was effectively a parliament of the armed forces, formed in order to prevent divisions within the military, of the kind that had led to the defeat of the attempted coup in 1960. This however was no coup, but rapidly developed into a full-scale revolution, comparable to those in France in 1789 or Russia in 1917. Revolutions have indeed characteristically occurred in decaying monarchies incapable of meaningful reform, and Ethiopia was no exception.[4] The overthrow of the reformist regime was prompted by its leader's attempt to promote a negotiated settlement to the conflict in Eritrea, to which the *Derg*, rigid in its militarised Ethiopian nationalism, was bitterly opposed. This was to set the tone for the regime that it established. The reformist general was killed, and immediately afterwards, over fifty leading officials of the imperial regime were summarily murdered. This action made brutally clear that there would be no turning back, and established a pattern of violence that later events reinforced.

The emergence of a government that was both revolutionary in policy and military in origin presented the student-led radicals who had led the destruction of the imperial regime with a dilemma: should they collaborate with the *Derg*, and seek to guide it in the process, or should they oppose it in the name of a genuine people's revolution? In the event, they split, bringing into the open a division within the student movement that had been growing over the previous decade. One faction, grouped under the leadership of the All Ethiopia Socialist Movement (generally known by its Amharic acronym as *Meison*), favoured collaboration with the military. This group also favoured an idea of Ethiopian nationalism that broadly corresponded to that of the *Derg*. The other, led by the Ethiopian People's Revolutionary Party (known by its English acronym as EPRP), denounced the *Derg* as 'Bonapartist', and vowed unrelenting opposition. It was correspondingly more prepared than *Meison* to acknowledge the need to represent the different 'nationalities' of which Ethiopia was composed. The result was the 'Red Terror', in which the EPRP and its enemies fought out a vicious campaign of assassination in the streets of Addis Ababa and other major towns. The EPRP was destroyed, with the survivors retreating to the countryside to pursue the apparently hopeless option of rural guerrilla warfare, while the *Derg* turned on its former allies in *Meison* and established its total supremacy. Within the *Derg* itself, factional conflicts invariably resulted in the killing of the losers, until a single strongman, Mengistu Haile-Mariam, came out on top, and the normal Ethiopian structure of autocratic rule was re-established.[5]

From this bloodbath there emerged by 1977 a powerful regime with a coherent response to the problems inherent in Ethiopia's make-up that its imperial predecessor had so evidently failed to tackle. This can be described as Jacobin, after the French revolutionaries of the early 1790s. At its core was an uncompromising Ethiopian nationalism, which would incorporate all Ethiopians on an equal basis into a revolutionary state from which the old structures of exploitation and repression had been removed. This placed it on a collision course with the insurgents in Eritrea, where a sense of nationhood deeply opposed to incorporation into Ethiopia had already become evident, and allowed only a military solution to the conflict. But to other subject nationalities, it had something to offer. It was underpinned by the land reform of 1975, which nationalised all land, urban and rural, and although this did not constitute that 'land to the tiller' that the student revolutionaries had demanded, it destroyed the landlord class imposed as a result of conquest on much of the highland periphery, and gave peasants a genuine stake in the regime. Land was thereafter allocated through peasants' associations set up throughout the countryside, while urban land was managed by urban dwellers' associations. Known as *kebelles*, these associations created a powerful structure of governance down to the very lowest level, which incorporated peasants especially into an administrative system of a kind that had never previously existed. Economic management at the macro level was straightforwardly state socialist, with nationalised private enterprises turned into state corporations. Large agricultural schemes, like the sugar and cotton estates run by Dutch and British companies in the Awash Valley, became state farms, and although collectivisation was avoided, 'villagisation' in the later 1980s concentrated previously scattered peasant homesteads, supposedly to provide services such as health and education, but in practice largely as a means of strengthening central control.[6]

While the Ethiopian revolution was almost entirely home-grown, international developments also turned in the regime's favour. In 1977, the Somali government took advantage of the domestic chaos created by the revolution to invade the Somali-inhabited area of Ethiopia, a catastrophic mistake that enabled the regime both to mobilise the support created by land reform to raise a large army, and to establish strong links with the Soviet bloc. Before the revolution, the USSR had provided extensive military aid to Somalia, as a counterweight to American support for Ethiopia, but—given the chance to establish itself in a much more powerful and strategically more important state, with an evidently genuine commitment to Soviet-style socialism—it switched alliances, giving the previously isolated Ethiopian regime a superpower backer, with virtually limitless quantities of military hardware at its disposal. The government's ability to raise a large army, fuelled by the enthusiasm created by land reform and backed by Soviet weaponry and a strike force of Cuban soldiers, enabled it to defeat the Somalis decisively in March 1978, setting in train the events that were to lead to the collapse of the Somali state. At the same time, Ethiopia became a fully-fledged member of the Soviet bloc, which was then, in the aftermath of American defeat in southeast Asia, enjoying a period of exceptional though short-lived global success. The *Derg* initially resisted Soviet pressure to establish a vanguard party modelled on the Communist Party of the Soviet Union, fearing that this might provide a vehicle for external control as had been the case in the satellite states of eastern Europe. Having taken steps to avoid this danger, it celebrated the tenth anniversary of the revolution in 1984 by inaugurating the Workers' Party of Ethiopia, which behind a Leninist façade was essentially the existing military leadership in civilian garb, while allowing some scope for the incorporation of subservient civilian ideologues.

The *Derg's* problem was that its project of seeking to establish a united, modernised and socialist Ethiopia, however intellectually coherent and forcibly imposed, simply did not work. At an economic level, this was hardly surprising. Top-down economic control was a failure in much the same way, and for much the same reasons, as it invariably proved elsewhere. State farms were particularly catastrophic, and suffered from the characteristic problems of socialist gigantism, wasting resources on machinery that soon lay rusting at the edges of massive fields that had been cleared with disastrous environmental consequences. The productive enterprise of supposedly liberated peasants was increasingly discouraged by exploitative state marketing organisations that extracted food at low prices to supply the towns and the army. A famine in 1984, though undoubtedly owing much to drought, drew embarrassing attention to the failure of the revolutionary regime to improve the condition of the peasantry, and forced it to look for relief food from western Europe and North America, since its Soviet ally was in no position to provide it.

More surprising, and ultimately fatal, was military failure. A concept of nationalism imposed from the top down inevitably involved a very substantial element of coercion, which a regime capable of raising an army variously estimated at up to half a million, and backed to the hilt by a military superpower, might well have been expected to be able to provide. That it was unable to do so was due not so much to the deficiencies of the Ethiopian army itself, which retained a remarkable level of competence and dedication, but to the quality of the resistance that it faced, especially in Eritrea. The initial opposition to Ethiopian rule in Eritrea had derived largely from the Muslim peoples of the western lowlands, who in any case had very little in common with the Ethiopian state. The first resistance movement, the Eritrean

Liberation Front (ELF), was largely Muslim in leadership and composition, and drew support from some of the more radical Arab regimes in the Middle East, especially Iraq and Syria. The end of federation in 1962 alienated precisely that group, the Tigrinya-speaking Christians of highland Eritrea, who had provided the main support for union with Ethiopia, but who also sought a significant level of autonomy from a regime in Addis Ababa with which they had little in common. Though membership never entirely corresponded with ethnicity or religion, these provided much of the backing for a new organisation, the Eritrean People's Liberation Front (EPLF), which was formally established in 1977, at precisely the time that the Red Terror was being fought out in Ethiopia.

The EPLF was to develop into one of the most formidable guerrilla insurgencies in the history of the world. The obstacles to its success were massive. It had to overcome not only the ethnic and religious diversity of Eritrea itself, which was divided equally between Muslims and Christians, but the differences between initially rival factions that coalesced to create it, with varying ideological and strategic approaches to the struggle against the vast and well-equipped Ethiopian army in which it was engaged. Its approach to the challenge of Eritrean nation-building was, like that of the *Derg* against which it was fighting, essentially Jacobin. Whereas earlier resistance movements had been broadly coalitional, seeking to put together alliances in which each of the main groups were represented, the EPLF sought to suppress any reference to ethnicity, race or religion, and to create instead a single and united Eritrean nation, forged in the heat of the struggle. Just as in Ethiopia, this raised issues not least of language, since Tigrinya was the language of the Christian highlanders, while Arabic tended to serve as a *lingua franca* for the different and linguistically more diverse Muslim groups. Over time, Tigrinya emerged as the dominant mode of communication, though its association with the Christians, who formed the preponderant group in the leadership, continued to cause problems. One unifying factor was that even though many of the leaders were highlanders, the war itself, especially in the critical formative stage, was fought very largely in the Muslim regions of Eritrea, and imposed a need to maintain the support of the local populations. Ideologically, the EPLF was explicitly Marxist, in contrast to the unspecific nationalism of earlier resistance groups, and it drew organisationally on the Chinese model. Its eventual leader, Isayas Afewerki, had received military and ideological training in China. The unity of the movement, and the acceptance of a ruthlessly centralised command structure, were likewise derived from sheer military necessity in the struggle against a formidable enemy.[7]

In 1977/78, when the *Derg* was preoccupied with the internal struggle for supremacy within Ethiopia and with the Somali invasion, the EPLF was able to achieve rapid success, and took control of much of Eritrea including many of the towns. In the process, it consolidated its position as the only effective Eritrean nationalist movement, and achieved an internal supremacy that was never seriously challenged. It was then faced by the need to confront the *Derg*. Following its victory against the Somalis, which had provided it both with a large and well-motivated army, and with Soviet support and weaponry, the *Derg* was then in a position to turn its attention to Eritrea. In the subsequent campaign in 1978–79, the EPLF, which at that stage had no weapons at its disposal remotely commensurate with those in the hands of its enemy, was obliged to abandon almost all of Eritrea's towns, and retreat to the thinly inhabited north and west. Under the headline, "Days of Remnants of Secessionist Bandits Lurking in Bushes Numbered",[8] the Ethiopian government confidently predicted victory. This was the period of most intense pressure, when the EPLF was able to develop its remarkable organisational and military skills. Given total Ethiopian command of the air, it was obliged to conduct much of its activity at night, and to move many of its resources underground, including its command centres, workshops, hospitals and training camps. The EPLF certainly benefitted from an open border with Sudan, which gave it tacit support in retaliation for Ethiopian backing for the SPLA insurgency in southern Sudan, and also from the large Eritrean diaspora, but this was in essence a domestic movement with a high level of self-reliance.

Against All Odds, to borrow the title of a book written by one of its Western supporters,[9] the EPLF managed to cling on. The last town of any significance remaining in its hands, Nacfa in the Sahel region of northern Eritrea, became the symbol of resistance, and was held against assaults that left massive casualties on both sides.[10] The most ambitious of the Ethiopian government's offensives, the Red Star Multifaceted Revolutionary Campaign, was launched amidst great fanfare in January 1982, and sought to combine the military defeat of the EPLF with rehabilitation and economic development campaigns—an attempt to win the support of civilian populations for which the moment had long passed. Ethiopian sources have it that this failed to take Nacfa only because Mengistu Haile-Mariam insisted that his own former division should have the honour of leading the army into the town, and that during the pause that resulted the EPLF managed to plug the gap in its defences. With the failure of the Red Star campaign, the EPLF was able to move gradually onto the strategic offensive, strengthened by captured weapons, including tanks, that enabled it (apart from air power) to match those at the government's disposal. The key breakthrough was the capture in March 1988 of the Ethiopian army's base at Afabet, which gave the EPLF huge quantities of material, including notably heavy artillery, and obliged the Ethiopians to withdraw from much of western Eritrea to concentrate on defending the highlands. The loss of the port of Massawa in February 1990, coupled with the success of the TPLF in the Tigray region immediately to the south of Eritrea, left the Ethiopian forces isolated. The war ended in May 1991, as the EPLF marched triumphantly into Asmara.

The second of the insurgencies that led to the fall of the *Derg*, and in this case formed the regime that replaced it, was conducted by the Tigray People's Liberation Front (TPLF). Despite obvious common interests in the defeat of the *Derg*, this group differed significantly from the EPLF in origins, aims and organisation. Whereas the EPLF derived from dissent within Eritrea that dated back to the federation period, the TPLF was formed as a result of the Ethiopian revolution, and specifically from the brutal authoritarianism of the *Derg*, which led a small group of Tigrayan students in Addis Ababa to conclude that their only hope lay in guerrilla warfare back in their home region. Whereas the EPLF sought to create a single and coherent Eritrean nationalism, the TPLF sought to mobilise the separate identities of the different 'nationalities' that comprised Ethiopia, in terms of the approach to the 'national question' articulated by some of the student radicals before 1974. And while the EPLF was rigidly hierarchical in structure, the TPLF—not least as a reflection of its own weakness—sought a more open and consensual movement linked to the needs of the Tigrayan peasantry.[11]

Even more than the EPLF in Eritrea, the TPLF was isolated from the outside world, and its first priority was to establish 'movement hegemony' in Tigray itself, against rivals launched both by the regional aristocracy which had ruled the region under Haile Sellassie, and by other Marxist groups. This, coupled with a total lack of military experience, called for a steep learning process, in which the TPLF benefitted from its open internal structure and especially the practice of *gim gima*, a discussion after each operation or when important decisions had to be made, designed to learn from mistakes and secure consensus over future policies. And although there was an obvious need to collaborate with the EPLF in opposition to the *Derg*, relations between the two movements were complex and at times hostile. The TPLF did not want to become a mere subordinate of the much more powerful EPLF, while the EPLF was suspicious of the TPLF's policies on the 'national question', which posed a threat to its very different approach in Eritrea. The TPLF also resorted to mobile guerrilla warfare, while the EPLF opted for a more conventional military strategy.

One source of lasting grievance was that an open division between the two movements coincided with the great famine of 1984/85, and led the EPLF to deny its Tigrayan counterpart access through Eritrea to relief supplies in Sudan. Both movements, and the *Derg*, ruthlessly used famine relief food to maintain political control, and this move was seen by the TPLF as an attempt to destroy its peasant base. The TPLF responded by building a road to Sudan without passing through Eritrea, and evacuating a large number of peasants to relief camps across the border. Relations between the TPLF and EPLF were restored in 1988, though they could never be as close as before, and the EPLF took a key role especially in battles around Endaselassie, the key army base in the region, in 1988/89.[12] This support was to have an important impact on the EPLF's assessment of its strength relative to the TPLF, and in turn on the Eritrea-Ethiopia war of 1998–2000, though the TPLF had also given vital support to the EPLF defence of Nacfa.[13] Defeat at Endaselassie led the *Derg* to withdraw from Tigray, leaving the TPLF facing a decision as to whether to consolidate its position in its homeland, or to advance on Addis Ababa and seek regime change. After prolonged internal debate, it opted for the second alternative, and started the long march south.

By this time, the regime's army had been obliged by previous losses to rely increasingly on forcibly conscripted and hastily trained troops, and its morale—after more than a decade of war-fare—was collapsing. The TPLF's advance was therefore much less bitterly contested than it had expected, and as increasing numbers of conscripts fell into its hands, it was able to use these to establish allied political movements in the regions from which they had come, in the process creating the Ethiopian Peoples' Revolutionary Democratic Front (EPRDF), the title under which the TPLF-led regime was to seize and exercise power. In May 1991, the previously unthinkable happened. As the TPLF approached Addis Ababa, the *Derg* leader Mengistu Haile-Mariam fled (to Zimbabwe, where he remains), and—four days after the EPLF had taken Asmara—this once tiny student-led guerrilla movement from the far north of the country marched almost unopposed into Addis Ababa, and established a new government.

The Death of the Somali Dream

The Somali-inhabited territories of the Horn could scarcely have been more different, socially and culturally, from Ethiopia and Eritrea, but they too followed a path that differed markedly from most of sub-Saharan Africa, in that it challenged the territorial structure of the state, and also resulted in failure. In the period immediately after the Second World War, all of the vast but sparsely inhabited Somali territories, save for the perennially anomalous French Somali Coast (now Djibouti), were controlled by the British, who in addition to the British Somaliland Protectorate and Kenya, held formerly Italian Somalia as an occupied enemy territory and continued to administer the Somali-inhabited area of Ethiopia. This induced the then British Foreign Secretary to propose an arrangement, known as the Bevin Plan, under which all the Somali lands would be grouped into a single entity. There is no reason to suppose that this was anything more than a pragmatic response to how to administer a distinctive and mobile people, and it had no chance of wider acceptance: it outraged the Ethiopians, who held sovereignty over the large territory known as the Ogaden, and was dismissed by the other great powers who, with the United Kingdom, were responsible for the fate of former Italian Somalia. The Somalis were reterritorialized, as Ethiopia reclaimed control of its own southeastern region, and the United Nations returned Somalia to the Italians, under a tightly constrained trusteeship administration. However, it helped to prompt a form of Somali nationalism which, unlike anywhere else in sub-Saharan Africa, was predicated on the union of Somalis across colonial-era territorial frontiers, rather than within the colonial grid.

The principal Somali nationalist movement, the Somali Youth League, was thus pan-Somali in organisation and policy, though it attracted support especially from the Darood clans, which constituted both the largest and the most widely spread of the Somali clan families, with representatives in Somalia, Kenya, Ogaden and British Somaliland. It assumed a dominant role in the Somalia trust territory, where it also enlisted the support of the Hawiye clans, and where the only opposition came from the Digil-Mirifle clans of the Webi Shebele and Juba river valleys. It spread into the Darood-inhabited eastern zone of the British protectorate, where the major party in a somnolent process of political mobilisation was the Somaliland National League, which represented especially the Isaaq clans. Popular pressure for Somali unification was so strong even in the protectorate, however, that the date of independence was advanced to 1960, when the Italian mandate in Somalia was due to expire, at which point the two territories united to form the Somali Republic.[14]

This exemplary democratic process inevitably reflected the values and identities of the pastoral society from which it derived. Members of parliament were elected essentially as the representatives of their clans, regardless of the party to which they formally belonged, and Somali governance—in the sharpest contrast to the autocratic hierarchy of the neighbouring Ethiopian empire—amounted in practice to endless negotiations over how to share the spoils of government between them. Since this system was founded on an underlying national identity, moreover, it could dispense with the highly personalised leadership and intolerance of dissent found in nationalist parties elsewhere in Africa whose principal *raison d'être* was the struggle against colonialism. As a result it was able—quite exceptionally in immediately post-independence Africa—to change both the prime minister and the president, peacefully and by constitutional means.

There were problems, certainly, not least in uniting two territories with different administrative systems, creating discontents especially in the former British protectorate, which as the smaller of the two had most to lose. Mogadishu became the national capital, with all the advantages that brought with it, while Hargeisa was reduced to the status of a provincial headquarters. The political scene was frequently chaotic. The major challenge, however, was that the unification of the two entirely Somali-inhabited territories promoted, but did nothing to realise, the republic's claims on the large Somali-inhabited regions of both Kenya and Ethiopia. These prompted a brief border clash with Ethiopia in March 1964, and the bitter 'shifta war' of 1963–67 in the Somali region of Kenya, when an attempt by Kenyan Somalis to join Somalia was brutally suppressed by the Kenyan army.

In order to pursue any plausible unification strategy, the republic needed both a much larger army than was needed for internal security, and external allies through whom to get the necessary arms and training; and in a strategically sensitive region, in which its putative opponents were strongly backed by the United States (in the case of Ethiopia), and the United Kingdom (for Kenya), an obvious resource lay in the Soviet Union. An initial military cooperation agreement with the USSR was signed in 1963, and subsequently much extended. In the midst of a political crisis in October 1969, prompted by the assassination of president Shirmarke, the army seized power in a classic *coup d'état,* and installed a military regime headed by its commanding officer, Muhammad Siyad Barre.

In the constant oscillation between solidarity and fragmentation that characterises Somali politics, the coup marked a shift towards the reassertion of a pan-Somali identity, in reaction against the clan-based squabbles of the civilian regime. The governing Supreme Revolutionary Council announced its commitment to 'scientific socialism' and its rejection of clan identities: a ceremony was held in which effigies representing the different clans were burned and buried. In marked contrast to Ethiopia, where scientific socialism or Marxism-Leninism had a deep resonance in perceptions of the country's social and political structure, it held little appeal for Somalis. Marxists have had considerable difficulty in incorporating pastoralist societies within an ideological framework that traces a developmental path from primitive communism through feudalism and capitalism to socialism and eventual full communism, and scientific socialism calls for no very evident policy trajectory for pastoralism, in contrast to a readily defined set of steps in societies of settlement: it is difficult to nationalise a camel. In the Somali case, its adoption may best be regarded firstly as a blueprint for creating a strong and centrally directed state, and secondly as a way to strengthen the alliance with the Soviet Union, from which the resources needed to build such a state would in large measure have to come.

The key objective towards which both the strong state and the Soviet alliance were directed, and on which the construction of a united Somali nationalism has historically been based, was the reclamation of the Somali-inhabited territories in Kenya and, especially, Ethiopia. The expulsion of the Russians from Egypt by Sadat in 1972 fortuitously gave Somalia a greatly enhanced strategic significance in Soviet eyes, reflected in large shipments of arms to Somalia, the expansion of the Somali army from 4,000 to 17,000 men, the deployment of about 3,600 Soviet advisers, many of them military, and the establishment of Soviet bases at Berbera on the Gulf of Aden and Kismayu near the Kenya border.[15] A Marxist-Leninist vanguard party, the Somali Revolutionary Socialist Party (SRSP) was created, though all of its politburo members were senior army officers. The 1969 coup was relabelled, somewhat presumptuously, the 'October Revolution'.

Though the Somali military build-up preceded the revolution in Ethiopia, this appeared to present a historic opportunity to achieve unification. The Ethiopian army was still larger than the Somali, but it was heavily engaged in Eritrea, and the United States had denied it weaponry of the calibre reaching the Somalis. Most important, the Ethiopian armed forces were deeply involved in the chaos and internal blood-letting that accompanied the revolution. Somali government support for an existing insurgency in Somali-inhabited Ethiopia, the Western Somali Liberation Front, was covertly stepped up, and escalated in 1977 into a full-scale invasion. As already noted, this was checked and then decisively reversed by the Ethiopian mobilisation and the Soviet switch of alliances.

The experience of the Siyad regime demonstrates the impossibility of constructing a powerful state on the foundations provided by a pastoralist society. Shorn of the unifying impetus provided by the war against Ethiopia, Somalia rapidly reverted to clan identities as the main bases for political action and identity. Siyad himself managed to survive attempts to oust him, and shored up his diminishing support through an alliance of three Darood clans: his father's clan, the Marehaan; his mother's clan, the Ogaden; and a related clan prominent in the eastern part of the former British protectorate, the Dulbahante—a trio commonly known by the acronym MOD. Unimportant members of other clans were given posts, in order to provide the appearance of a broader base, and Somali politics thereafter consisted in the manipulation of clan rivalries around a steadily shrinking constituency for the regime. The control of Mogadishu by the Hawiye presented a particular threat, and it was from these that the clan-based militias that were eventually to overthrow Siyad came.

The post-war fragmentation of Somali politics was particularly significant for the former British Somaliland. As already noted, this had a core Isaaq population in the centre of the territory, controlling the major towns of Hargeisa, Berbera and Burao, with Darood clans in the east of the territory and a Dir clan, the Gadabursi, in the west. As the part of Somalia with the strongest sense of having lost out from unification in 1960, this was in any event likely opposition territory, which the regime's association with the Darood could only intensify. The Isaaq also had long-standing differences with the Ogaden, part of the core MOD constituency, over grazing rights. Brutal repression of protests in the north, including a student demonstration known as 'the day of throwing stones', had its usual counterproductive impact. This led in 1981 to the launch in London of a primarily Isaaq resistance, the Somali National Movement (SNM). Another opposition grouping, the Somali Salvation Democratic Front (SSDF), was dominated by the Majerteen clan of the Darood, prominent in the extreme north-east of Somalia, who subsequently played a leading role in launching the quasi-state of Puntland.

As was only to be expected, these groups gained support from the *Derg* regime in Ethiopia, and launched attacks which resulted in further repression, including extensive bombing. The *Derg*'s defeat at Afabet in Eritrea in 1988 appeared to offer Siyad a way out, since Mengistu badly needed to shore up his northern front, and agreed a deal with Siyad under which each undertook to stop supporting the other's rebels, and to expel them from their territories. Faced by this threat, the SNM took the risky and costly option of launching an all-out attack on Siyad's forces in northern Somalia, which succeeded in capturing Burao and large areas of Hargeisa, prompting a bombing campaign that may have killed as many as 60,000 people, and cemented an intense hostility towards government from Mogadishu that was to lead to the formation of the republic of Somaliland. Hargeisa was virtually destroyed, by aircraft taking off from the government airbase in Hargeisa itself. When Siyad was eventually ousted in January 1991, by a militia drawn from a coalition of Hawiye clans and called the United Somali Congress, the SNM took over most of the former British protectorate, and declared it an independent republic.

The region's perennial outlier, initially known as the French Somali Coast, had meanwhile followed an altogether more conventional path. Having voted overwhelmingly to stay with France under de Gaulle's referendum of 1958, it remained a French possession after all the other French colonies in Africa became independent in 1960. In a further referendum in 1967, it opted for continued though looser association with France, though with a name change to French Territory of the Afars and Issas, both reflecting recognition of the Afar, who broadly inhabit the area to the north of the Gulf of Tajura and had voted strongly in favour of the French relationship, and displacing the name Somali (with its overtones of identity with the other Somali populations of the Horn, and thus of potential inclusion within a united Somali state) by that of the principal Somali clan. Formal independence in 1977, precisely coinciding with the Somali-Ethiopian war, was accompanied by a continuing French military presence and security guarantee that (despite clashes with Eritrea and a civil conflict in 1991–94) insulated what then became the republic of Djibouti from the conflicts endemic to the region. Its increasingly significant interactions with the rest of the region are examined later.

1991: Year Zero in the Horn

The analysis of post-independence African states, and especially of their failures, has often—understandably enough—started from an emphasis on the *externalities* of their creation and maintenance.[16] These states, after all, had overwhelmingly been created from the outside, by a European colonialism that had divided the continent through an astonishingly arbitrary process in which indigenous peoples had virtually no part, into territories with artificial boundaries that grouped often entirely different peoples under a common jurisdiction. When these territories subsequently emerged as independent states, they had little to hold them together beyond continuity and the experience of a common colonial rule. Many of the peoples involved had no previous experience of statehood at all, and the state itself had to be 'grafted', in Bayart's expressive phrase,[17] onto the rootstock provided by indigenous social norms and structures. It was little wonder that the rulers of such states had to resort to governing them by methods commonly described as 'neo-patrimonial', through a mixture of force and deals done with those who controlled significant sources of influence, in ways that militated against effective development programmes and readily lent themselves to corruption. Given that the economies of these states were highly dependent on the export of primary commodities, the prices of which were subject to wild and unpredictable fluctuation, the resources in the hands of local rulers were extremely volatile, further complicating the problems of governance, and frequently subjecting them to external control, most obviously in the form of the 'structural adjustment programmes' imposed by international financial institutions from the late 1970s onwards. This entire process was aptly described by Bayart as one of 'extraversion'.

Many of these characteristic features of African statehood applied equally to the Horn. Its boundaries were scarcely less artificial than those of other states in Africa, the straight lines demarcating the Somali territories being especially revealing. Eritrea and Ethiopia incorporated very different peoples, notably in each case both highland agriculturalists and lowland pastoralists. And while the highlanders had powerful state traditions, the pastoralists— and especially the Somali—had virtually none. Their economies scarcely differed, save in their poverty, lack of development, and absence of significant mineral resources, from those of the rest of Africa. Their external dependence was particularly acute in the sphere of armaments, both Ethiopia and Somalia attracting levels of superpower military support that most of the rest of Africa was spared, and that did them both a vast amount of damage. The impact of these common elements in the Horn was nonetheless distinctive. In Somalia, the attempt to construct a powerful state on the fragile basis of a pastoralist society, through which to pursue the project of national unity, not only challenged the regional and continental order in a way that no other independent African state has sought to do, but had a catastrophic impact on the Somali state itself. In Ethiopia, the state itself survived its abuse at the hands of the *Derg* regime, but at the cost of exposing the deep limitations in its concept of nationhood. In each case, it was the indigenous dynamic, rather than the externalities of statehood, that most evidently led to disaster.

By 1991, the patterns of state formation established by empire and revolution in Ethiopia, and by the post-colonial transition in the peripheral territories of the Horn, had comprehensively failed. In January 1991 in Somalia, and just four months later in Ethiopia, the established and extremely authoritarian regimes in what were then the two principal states of the Horn were not merely overthrown, but destroyed by armed insurgencies. This confronted the region's peoples and political actors with the task of establishing some new kind of political order in four different territories, since the new regimes in both Eritrea and former British Somaliland (hence forth called simply Somaliland, as

61

distinct from the former Italian territory now referred to as Somalia) rejected any continued association with the regimes based in Addis Ababa and Mogadishu. Strikingly, the effect of state failure was to re-establish the former territorial structure of the Horn, created by colonialism and then dissolved in the quest for unification in the era of decolonisation. At the time of African independence, it was sometimes suggested that the artificial state structure established by colonialism might be expected to give way, over the course of time, to a new territorial order derived from the identities of indigenous African societies. In the two cases in the continent, both in the Horn, in which some process of this kind, however flawed, was undertaken, the effect was just the opposite; and while division on the basis of the colonial frontiers was certainly encouraged, especially in the case of Somaliland, by the enhanced chances of recognition if it followed the territorial logic of existing African states, this was by no means all of the story. Especially in Eritrea, the colonial partition had acquired a legitimacy of its own.

The task of reconstructing a political order had to be undertaken, if indeed it was to be possible at all, under conditions of intense conflict and state breakdown. All of the new regimes that sought to achieve it came fresh to the task of creating and governing a state, having previously operated as armed insurgencies. Their power derived from the barrel of a gun, and such organisation and legitimacy as they possessed derived from the structures needed to fight a war, and from the relationships that they had been able to build with the inhabitants of the areas in which they fought. They faced an extremely daunting task, and one that was conceived and tackled quite differently in Eritrea, Ethiopia, Somalia, Somaliland, and indeed Djibouti. The remaining chapters will seek to examine how this process took place in each of the territories concerned, why it took the form that it did, how it related to their underlying social and governance structures, and the consequences for the resulting states individually, for the relationships between them, and for the political structures of the Horn as a whole.

3

STATE RECONSTRUCTION IN ETHIOPIA

A New Kind of Ethiopia?

The TPLF's takeover of state power in Ethiopia in May 1991 was remarkably smooth, as the guerrilla army from distant Tigray, many of its soldiers little more than children, slid into Addis Ababa and took over key installations in the city against minimal opposition. Fears of a collapse into chaos, like that after the fall of the Siyad regime in Mogadishu a few months earlier, were rapidly put to rest. Ethiopians retain a pragmatic approach to authority—as an Amhara proverb has it, 'The sun that rises tomorrow will be our sun; the government that rules tomorrow will be our government'—and the new regime could draw on the same deference to those who hold power as its predecessor. The once formidable army of the *Derg* in large measure demobilised itself; conscripts could be seen selling their Kalashnikovs on the streets of Addis Ababa, in order to raise the money with which to pay their bus fare home. The extension of the new government's control into the rest of the country, where most of the population had virtually no idea of who these new rulers were, for the most part went equally smoothly. Most strikingly of all, the monthly civil service salaries, due just a few days after the takeover, were paid in full and on time.

This points to a vital difference between the Ethiopian experience, and that of the other insurgents who were seizing political power almost throughout the Horn at much the same time. The TPLF did not find themselves confronted by a *tabula rasa* of the kind that faced their contemporaries in the Somali territories and Eritrea. Instead, they inherited a *state*—a deeply problematic state to be sure, and one which would need to be reoriented away from the role that it had played under the *Derg*, but a structured organisation of government nonetheless. Civil servants stayed at their posts, and transferred their allegiance to the new regime, as indeed they had done when the imperial government collapsed in 1974. And this was not just a matter of bureaucrats in Addis Ababa. It encompassed a hierarchy of rule that extended all the way down to the *kebelle*, the peasants' associations and urban dwellers' associations established during the revolution that remained in place as the base units of administration. The TPLF had indeed established similar institutions, known as *baito*, in the areas of Tigray that it had controlled during the guerrilla war, and it readily adopted their equivalents in the rest of the country. A state, of course, is not a neutral instrument of power, but one that carries with it its own interests and attitudes, and imposes significant constraints on those who seek to use it; but these were, on the whole, strengthening constraints, that enabled a movement that had until recently been fighting a guerrilla war in the distant mountains of Tigray to adapt to the very different challenges of running the government of a large and diverse country, most of which was completely unknown to its new rulers. They could not have managed without it.

One straightforward initial decision was the immediate and unqualified recognition of Eritrea's right to full independence. This was indeed a *fait accompli*. The EPLF declined any opportunity to participate in the government of the rest of Ethiopia, of which Eritrea was still at that moment formally a part, and instead immediately started to act as though it were already the government of an independent state, a status that was formalised following a referendum two years later. Some unreconstructed unionists in Addis Ababa and among the Ethiopian diaspora accused the new regime of having 'given away' Eritrea, an assertion that flew in the face of the situation on the ground. There were inevitably to be problems in Ethiopia's relations with Eritrea, which indeed turned out to be far greater than can plausibly have been expected at the time, but the union with Eritrea had proved to be a burden that had cost appalling numbers of lives on both sides, and from which Ethiopia—regardless of future events—could now mercifully be relieved.

But this still left the TPLF with an urgent need to construct a domestic political settlement. Its existing political base was a very narrow one indeed, derived only from the legitimacy that it had unquestionably built among the people of Tigray, a small and deeply undeveloped region in the far north of the country, and from the credit that it could claim for having liberated the rest of the country from the oppressive and by this time almost universally detested rule of the *Derg*. But this did not amount to the entitlement to rule that most 'liberation movements', from the EPLF in Eritrea to the ANC in South Africa, are able to claim from their leadership of a nationwide liberation struggle. Instead, it left the regime with a major task of coalition-building on its hands, through which to build linkages with the vast majority of Ethiopians outside Tigray. This likewise served as a strengthening constraint, in that the very weakness of its title to rule forced it to engage in political processes, and notably in coalition-building, for which victorious liberation movements generally feel no need, but which are central to the construction of a viable political order.

It was in any case clear that the model of Ethiopian 'nation-building' that had been implicit in the country's approach to governance, from Menilek to Mengistu, through the imposition of a top-down hierarchy by whatever level of coercion was required, had been tested to destruction under the *Derg*. The new government needed to set about a substantive reconstruction of the Ethiopian state. Though it was difficult to envisage the instant emergence of liberal multi-party democracy in a country whose political traditions had been so consistently authoritarian, something more consensual was evidently required. To this task the TPLF brought the approach articulated by one strand of the student Marxist intelligentsia during the pre-revolutionary period, and derived from—of all people—Joseph Stalin. Designed to fit the ethnic composition of Russia, and not entirely implausible in its application to Ethiopia, this called for the recognition and right to self-determination of all the 'nations, nationalities and peoples' within the boundaries of the state. In striking contrast to post-colonial African states, which took the imposed territorial structure as a given, this—paradoxically, in Africa's only 'non-colonial' state—denied the legitimacy of the means by which that state had been constructed, and sought (in principle, at least) to build up from its indigenous ethnicities, seen as the building blocks on which the state had to be founded. The coalition parties that were created to form the Ethiopian Peoples' Democratic Revolutionary Front (or EPRDF), as the new ruling party was called, were therefore constructed (like the TPLF itself) on an explicitly ethnic basis. Implicit in this approach, and indeed in Marxist approaches to ethnicity as a whole, ethnic attachments were viewed as nothing more than suppressed ideologies of class struggle, derived from relationships of exploitation that took on a fortuitously ethnic colouring. This too was a feature of the Russian archetype that could plausibly be extended to Ethiopia, given especially the nature of the late nineteenth century imperial expansion, and the inequalities that resulted from it. It implied in turn that once the basic problem of exploitation had been addressed, the ethnic consciousness that derived from it would automatically wither away. Only Marxists will be surprised that this assumption turned out to be mistaken.

A third strengthening constraint that helped to shape the EPRDF regime as it took over power was its relationship to the international order, both continental and global. Whereas the other victorious movements of 1991 had to establish their foreign policies virtually from scratch, and in the case of Somalia rapidly became the object of external intervention rather than being able to create a foreign policy at all, the new government of Ethiopia found itself already embedded in international politics. Addis Ababa was the headquarters not only of the Organisation of African Unity (which some years later was to become the African Union), but of a range of other international organisations, notably the United Nations Economic Commission for Africa. Ethiopia as a state had an exceptional level of diplomatic exposure, and a diplomatic corps unequalled in the continent. This certainly imposed constraints, in that the new regime had to accept norms of continental diplomacy, and fit itself into the global order created by the end of the Cold War and the apparent dominance of the Western alliance, even though its own ideological orientation was heavily Marxist and it had emerged from an experience of revolutionary guerrilla warfare that in central America or southeast Asia had been virtually coterminous with hostility to the United States. Ethiopian diplomats, too, would need to adapt to a government with very different ideas from its predecessor. But equally, the regime would be greatly strengthened by its ability to build both continental and global alliances, and possessed a leadership capable of appreciating the requirements for doing so.

The TPLF's leader and chief ideologist, Meles Zenawi, came to figure as the philosopher-king of the EPRDF regime. A man of quite extraordinary intelligence, Meles[1] had been a medical student in Addis Ababa at the time when, early in the revolution, he fled the city in order to help set up a guerrilla insurgency in his home region.[2] He was not the original leader of the TPLF, which insisted on collective leadership and initially alternated the chairmanship between two other members, Aregowie Berhe and Sebhat Nega,[3] nor was he especially prominent in the military campaign. He rose through intellectual ability, combined with an open-minded pragmatism in responding to events, though always within a Marxist frame of reference. He was no liberal democrat, and his conception of democracy derived from the Leninist vanguard model, but he had a remarkable capacity to articulate policy options and learn from his mistakes. Though the Horn of Africa imposes massive constraints on anyone in positions of power, Meles was far better able to overcome these than most, and the EPRDF regime was in large measure his construction, even though for the first decade after the takeover he was effectively the first among equals in what remained a collective leadership. At the same time, he was articulate and personally charming, and ideally equipped to build relations with the outside world.

In the immediate aftermath of victory, the new rulers convened a conference of the major opposition movements against the *Derg*, which drew up a Transitional Charter, committing the regime to decentralisation of the state, democratisation of the political structure, and liberalisation of the economy. These were all relatively uncontentious tasks, given both the need to reverse the political and economic state centralism of the previous regime, and the global context after the collapse of the Soviet Union and the end of the Cold War, but they allowed for a great deal of latitude in their actual implementation. The EPRDF was a very rare liberation movement, in that it came to power—thanks in large measure to Meles Zenawi—with a relatively coherent idea of what it wanted to achieve and how it proposed to go about it, and as the only participant with both power and an agenda, emerged from the conference with the blueprint that it had sought. Reviving an approach first articulated by a strand in the student movement before the 1974 revolution, this was to reconstruct Ethiopia as a federal state, in which the constituent units would be the country's ethnic groups, each of which would have a right to self-determination, and be represented by its own indigenous leadership. The crux lay in how this leadership would be chosen, and in the great majority of cases, there was little alternative on the ground to the parties that the EPRDF had already started to form under its own umbrella. There had been no opportunity to establish any rival to the *Derg* before May 1991, and for most of the country's nationalities, the chance to have their own parties offered opportunities well beyond anything that they had previously possessed, and would only be welcomed.

There were two significant exceptions. The first were the Amhara, who viewed themselves as the country's historic rulers, and many of whom were deeply sceptical about the 'balkanisation' of Ethiopia into separate ethnic units, and the dangers of division and fragmentation that this involved. It was noted that the Soviet model from which the new system derived had life only after death: the division into 'union republics' that had been meaningless so long as the USSR remained in place then served as the basis for creating fifteen independent states when it collapsed. The system of ethnic federalism carried the same dangers for Ethiopia. On the other hand, the Amhara were strongly associated with the state, and had no alternative organisation through which to promote their goals. It was however symptomatic that the party through which they participated in the EPRDF coalition was initially called the Ethiopian People's Democratic Movement (EPDM), indicating a national rather than ethnic identity, and only later was it retitled the Amhara National Democratic Movement (ANDM).

Table 2: Ethiopia: Population by Region and Ethnicity, 2007

Region			Ethnicity		
Tigray	4,316,988	5.8%	Oromo	25,363,765	34.4%
Afar	1,390,273	1.9%	Amhara	19,878,199	27.0%
Amhara	17,221,976	23.3%	Somali	4,586,976	6.2%
Oromia	26,993,933	36.6%	Tigray	4,486,513	6.1%
Somali	4,445,219	6.0%	Sidama	2,951,889	4.0%
Benishangul	784,345	1.1%	Gurage	1,859,831	2.5%
Southern	14,929,548	20.2%	Welayta	1,676,128	2.3%
Gambela	307,096	0.4%	Afar	1,276,867	1.7%
Harer	183,415	0.2%	Hadiya	1,269,382	1.7%
Addis Ababa	2,739,551	3.7%	Gamo	1,104,360	1.5%
Dire Dawa	341,834	0.5%	75 other groups under 1 million		
Special Area*	96,754	0.1%			
TOTAL	73,750,932				

*This is a largely Somali-inhabited area, enumerated separately from the Somali region.
Source: Ethiopia Census 2007.

The second and much more problematic exception were the Oromo, who had every reason to welcome a political order that rested on ethnic groups of which their own was the largest, but for whom there already existed an organisation, the Oromo Liberation Front (OLF), that claimed to represent the Oromo, and had established itself both in the diaspora and by limited and generally ineffective resistance within Ethiopia. The EPRDF, however, favoured its own Oromo wing, the Oromo People's Democratic Organisation (OPDO), and was not prepared to admit the claims of the OLF to become the designated representative of the Oromo. Whatever the justifications for this stance, and the OLF was poorly organised, lacked coherent policies, and made demands that were difficult to reconcile with the rights of other groups, this was effectively the test of whether the EPRDF was willing to work with autonomous organisations not under its own control. It soon became clear that the answer to this question was No. The OLF left the transitional government, and although its attempts at armed resistance were easily suppressed, it retained among many Oromos the sense that it was the only genuine representative of the Oromo people. Despite the government's claims that OPDO were the authentic voice of the Oromo peasantry, and that the OLF was no more than a thinly rooted group of intellectuals, this left a lasting weakness in the political base of the regime.

One critical issue created by a political structure of the kind that the new regime sought to set up was the territorialisation of ethnicity. Once the ethnic group is conceived as a unit of government, it must be provided with a specific territory which is governed by that group, and within which its members have at least an implicit status that is denied to those who do not belong to it. Given that Ethiopia, like the great majority of states both in Africa and throughout the world, had experienced over the years a great deal of population movement, intermingling and conquest, this was a very sensitive issue. The Boundary Commission established by the Transitional Government in 1991 to a significant extent took over, for lack of other options, the map drawn up by the Institute for the Study of Ethiopian Nationalities, a body established in the later years of the *Derg* regime, once it had recognised that ethnicities were not simply going to wither away, and that its own survival would require at least some recognition of ethnic variance. In the event, the Institute was able to do little beyond an initial mapping enterprise, based primarily on language, before the regime that had set it up was swept away, leaving its labours to have a much greater impact than had ever been envisaged by its founders.

Inevitably, this was a rough and ready business. Some groups, like the Amhara, formed a relatively compact block, whereas Oromia stretched from the frontiers of South Sudan in the west to Kenya in the south, and nearly as far as Somaliland in the east, leaving large intermediate areas inhabited by other peoples. The tiny Adere group in the city of Harer gained a region of their own, while the pastoralists along the frontier with the Sudans were combined into two multi-ethnic regions, of which Gambela, divided between Anywaa and Nuer, was the most contentious. The multi-ethnic commercial centre of DireDawa had to be brought under federal jurisdiction, and Addis Ababa was likewise designated as a federal territory, which formed an island within Oromia. Most complex of all was the southwestern region with its numerous small groups, which were eventually lumped together under the cumbersomely named Southern Nations, Nationalities and Peoples Regional State (SNNPRS), with separate sub-regions for the main groups within it. There was some opportunity for public consultation: the Siltie, previously regarded as a sub-group of the Gurage, overwhelmingly opted in a referendum for a separate status within the SNNPRS.[4] An attempt to combine four distinct but related peoples in the Southern Region—the Welayta, Gamu, Gofa and Dawro—into a single region with a composite language (to be called Wogagoda) aroused overwhelming opposition and was abandoned. The ecological frontier between pastoralists and settled agriculturalists remains an area of continuous contention.

As entrenched in the Constitution of the Federal Democratic Republic of Ethiopia (FDRE), promulgated in 1995, citizenship is vested primarily in the 'nations, nationalities and peoples' of which the republic is composed, each of which formally retains, under article 39(1), "an unconditional right to self-determination, including the right to secession".[5] What this might entail has yet to be tested, and it is evidently the intention of the EPRDF that

it never should be; the Constitution imposes procedural constraints which could be used to block any attempted secession
that was opposed by the central government. Whereas some
groups, such as the Somalis and the other peoples of the lowland
peripheries, could conceivably vote to leave Ethiopia and join
Somalia, Kenya, either of the Sudans or Eritrea, no plausible
option is open to most of the Southern peoples, while an Oromo
secession would entail the dissolution of Ethiopia. At a political
level, a significant division is implicit in the structure of the ruling party. While parties representing the sedentary highland
peoples of Ethiopia—the TPLF for Tigray, ANDM for Amhara,
OPDO for Oromia, and the Southern Ethiopian Peoples' Democratic Movement (SEPDM) for the Southern region—are full
members of the EPRDF, the parties representing the pastoralists,
such as the Somali, the Afar, and the inhabitants of Gambela and
Benishangul-Gumuz, have only an affiliated status. These are
regions historically marginalised and deeply undeveloped, which
would have had considerable difficulty in creating the governmental structures, and finding the appropriately qualified indigenous
citizens, needed to replicate the administrations of the four highland zones, and some level of external management would have
been needed to enable them to fit into the devolved structures
envisaged by the constitution. In addition, this peculiar and
somewhat invidious distinction appears to reflect the difficulties
already referred to in articulating pastoralism within Marxist
theory. It also relegates pastoralists to a subsidiary role in formal
government decision-making, though whether this makes any
practical difference is a separate question.

Creating a Managed Political Order

The political structure established in 1991 has survived, at the
time of writing in 2016, for a quarter of a century, making it (next

after the restored imperial government of 1941–1974) the second longest-lived Ethiopian regime of the last two hundred years. Though longevity certainly cannot be equated with stability, as the fate of the Haile Sellassie government makes all too clear, it does at least represent relative success in managing a complex and often conflict-ridden political system. With the death of its founding leader, Meles Zenawi, in 2012, and the peaceful and constitutional succession of Hailemariam Desalegn, it also achieved one of the most difficult tasks facing any political system, particularly in a state historically dependent on strong leadership. It has likewise carried out a substantive reconfiguration of the Ethiopian state, and presided over a long period of rapid economic growth. This is, in short, a regime to be taken seriously.

At the core of Ethiopian governance lie the problems of reconciling the three disparate elements that it embodies. The first of these is the historic structure of statehood, with both the ethnic disparities that it involves, and the entrenched conceptions of hierarchy and authority that have long been embedded in it. The second is the role of the armed movement that took over the government in 1991, the TPLF, which inevitably brought with it a power base that would continue to be highly influential in running whatever government it established. And the third is the evident need to broaden representation in government, and access to it, in such a way as to mitigate and in time remove the deep structural weaknesses embodied in Ethiopian statehood itself. Though the new regime showed itself to be thoroughly aware of this need, and rapidly developed constitutional and governmental structures designed to tackle it, it would be a very different matter actually to achieve the level of participation that ethnic federalism promised, given not least the threat that this would present both to existing ideas of statehood and to the continuing influence of the individuals and organisation that had effectively captured the state in 1991.

STATE RECONSTRUCTION IN ETHIOPIA

The system of governance developed over the subsequent quarter-century is best described as a managed political order, which seeks to provide an outlet for a level of participation and representation, but which at the same time is regulated to the level required to avoid any effective challenge to the leadership. It cannot remotely be described as democratic, in the liberal sense of the term that insists on open competition between rival political parties, the choice and change of ruling parties in free and fair elections, and respect for globally defined human rights. The sense of 'democracy' that it embodies is a strictly Leninist one, in which the ruling party enjoys an effective monopoly of political power, and seeks to incorporate within it what are taken to be the leading elements (or vanguard) of the society. Its aspirations are explicitly hegemonic, and challenges to its control have been suppressed with whatever level of force has been required for the purpose. Whether any more open and participatory system could at the same time be combined most obviously with the maintenance of basic peace and security, and more broadly with the levels of development that the regime has succeeded in bringing about, are deeply contested questions. The EPRDF regime remains a classic case of 'illiberal state-building',[6] in which acceptance of the regime's hegemony and its programme for the political and economic reconstruction of Ethiopia is a prerequisite for participation in government. The challenge that it faces is not only one of whether it can make this programme 'work', but of whether, in doing so, it can maintain an adequate basis of political support.

In every regime, worldwide, that has historically derived its power from liberation war, the legacy of the struggle has remained central to the effective exercise of power at least for so long as the generation engaged in that struggle remains on the political scene, and in some cases—as in China, for example—for several generations afterwards. In this respect, the continued centrality of the TPLF in Ethiopia is entirely normal. The difference lies in the fact that for most such regimes, the role of 'struggle credentials' is overt and indeed publicly glorified. In Ethiopia on the other hand, the inability of the 'liberators' to present their struggle as a fully national one, given that it emanated from such a small region of the country, has required them to articulate a nationwide programme of enhanced participation that threatened not only the historic structure of the Ethiopian state, but also their own tenure of power. In practice, it should therefore be no surprise that the formal mechanisms of government should be underpinned, and in the process subverted, by informal ones that continue to reflect the origins of the regime. This is, indeed, a thoroughly familiar feature of highland Ethiopian culture, characteristically expressed in the metaphor of 'wax and gold'.[7]

A Tigrayan thread correspondingly runs through Ethiopian governance, and though diluted since the death of Meles Zenawi in 2012 and the succession of a Welayta, Hailemariam Desalegn, it is still visible, notably in the security services. At a popular level, the regime is still perceived as essentially a Tigrayan one, and it is commonly assumed that any Tigrayan in the upper ranks of an organisation will enjoy privileged access to people in power, and may indeed represent the actual power structure in the organisation concerned, regardless of its formal hierarchy. The openness of the TPLF prior to 1991, when it permitted a level of discussion and debate quite exceptional for any liberation movement, continues to be reflected in a lively internal politics, quite at variance from that found in other member-parties of the EPRDF coalition. This was evident at the time of a serious split within the party in 2001, discussed later, and in open debate at the TPLF congress in 2015.

At the same time, not only has the need for a broader distribution of power been formalised in what in Nigerian parlance would be described as 'federal character' practices, but individuals from other parts of the country have come to assume a level of prominence that reflects the need to ensure that major constituencies are actually represented in central government. One of these is that each of the four major regions (i.e. those whose governing party is a full member of the EPRDF, Amhara, Oromo, Southern and Tigray), other than that of the Prime Minister, has a deputy Prime Minister, who serves in effect as the senior representative of the region in central government.[8] Leadership of each of the major groupings is balanced between the deputy Prime Minister in Addis Ababa, and the regional president within the region itself. Government ministries are likewise broadly shared between the major coalition parties, though given that leading politicians are effectively co-opted, there is no assurance that they actually represent their nominal constituencies in any meaningful way. Oromo representation is especially weak.

Within these constraints, nonetheless, visible changes have taken place in the historically hierarchical structures of Ethiopian governance. The most striking, at regional level, is that government offices are staffed by individuals indigenous to the area involved, and speaking the languages of the governed. In Ethiopian terms, this is revolutionary. In previous eras, Amharic was the language of government, and the representatives of the state were simply, for the most part, assumed to be Amhara, even though in many cases they were individuals of other origins who had taken on the cultural elements associated with Ethiopian statehood. The extent to which these individuals are representative of the peoples whom they govern is less certain: appointments continue to be managed essentially through the party structure, obedience to which is essential. Even so, the fact that officials generally come from local societies means that they are associated with elements or factions within those societies that in turn open up linkages between rulers and ruled that had previously been suppressed or non-existent. Over time, these have been mobilised to create patronage networks within each of the regions, and to gain control over resources, that by 2016 had come to impose very significant pressures on the central government, and indeed to threaten the structure of governance itself. These are considered in a later section.

Political processes in the highland regions have been shaped both by the structural characteristics of the regions themselves, and by their relationships to the EPRDF. Politics in Tigray, as already noted, has enjoyed a level of openness that reflected the continuing TPLF tradition of open discussion and debate that derived from the liberation war, together with the high level of factionalism to which the region has historically been liable. Levels of dissent have been permissible within the TPLF that would not have been tolerated elsewhere. At the other extreme, politics in Oromia has been affected both by the divergences between different parts of the region, and by the underlying weakness of support for the government, indicated especially by frequent outbreaks of violent protest, initially largely by students and schoolchildren, but gaining significantly in strength in 2015 and 2016. This has made it far harder for the EPRDF to recruit local leaders who can combine some standing in regional politics with the necessary level of acquiescence in central policy, hence one can gain local credibility only by advocating a level of Oromo autonomy that is seen as threatening by the central government. One indicator of the differences between the two regions is that during their respective party congresses in 2015, the TPLF meeting continued for two days, including debates over the readmission of a group who had been important during the liberation struggle but who had been sidelined by Meles, whereas the equivalent OPDO congress took no more than half a day, and was essentially formal. The politics of the Southern region inevitably turns to a large extent on competition between the different individual ethnicities that comprise it, and especially between the two largest groups, the Sidama, who also host the regional capital at Awassa, and the Welayta, the group to which Prime Minister Hailemariam Desalegn belongs. It provides a sharp reminder of the level of repression underlying the system that when, in 2002, a peaceful demonstration was organised by Sidama, to protest against a plan that would have separated Awassa from the Sidama zone and given it a special status separate from any specific group within the region, government forces opened fire on it with automatic weapons.[9]

The lowland regions have no prominent representative in the federal government who might correspond to the status of the deputy Prime Minister in the highland ones, and their regional presidents are likewise weaker. Their politics is most visible in internally divided regions. In the Gambela region, the historically most prominent group were the Anywaa (or Anuak), who therefore regarded themselves as the 'owners' of the region, and thus entitled to the leading role in its government. Over time, however, they have come under increasing pressure from the Nuer, an expanding group, by far the greater part of whose population has historically inhabited what is now South Sudan. Here, the transition from the *Derg* to the EPRDF, which for the most part went relatively smoothly, was particularly violent, since the Anywaa took advantage of the change of regime to attack both highland settlers, many of whom fled, and Nuer, who had benefitted from the *Derg*'s covert support for the SPLM in Southern Sudan.[10] With the post-independence upheavals in South Sudan, increasing numbers of Nuer have crossed into Ethiopia, challenging the place of the Anywaa in regional politics, and prompting conflict also between different Nuer groups. Somali politics is characteristically factionalised, notably as between the Ogaden clan as the largest in the Somali region, and a large number of other clans, in which the government with varying levels of success has sought to provide each clan with a level of representation broadly corresponding to its size, while simultaneously seeking to manage or manipulate clan (and sub-clan) politics in such a way as to limit the level of conflict and especially opposition to the centre.[11] However chaotic and sometimes violent this process may have been, the key change is that for the first time there *was* a political process, through which support on the ground could be translated into an official position of influence in regional and in some degree national politics. In this respect, local politics in Ethiopia has come closer—albeit only partially and unevenly—to the patterns familiar since the pre-independence era in formerly colonial territories such as Kenya.

While local political processes have thus developed under the federal system, to an extent that was not previously possible under either imperial or *Derg* regimes, Ethiopia thus remains well short of the levels of political openness and organisation permissible in African states with multi-party regimes, even those in which the ruling party has imposed a level of predominance that enables it to be reasonably confident of retaining control of the central government. Most strikingly, none of the regional governments, even the most marginal, have come even close to falling under the control of any party not belonging, or affiliated, to the EPRDF. However, although acceptable political activity is restricted to what can be maintained within the EPRDF party structure, this structure itself has become progressively loosened as regional politicians responded to demands arising from the base, and have in turn sought to manage such demands in order to strengthen their position at the centre. This process in turn has resulted in factional struggles within the regional parties, characterised by a complex mixture of person rivalries, popular mobilisation, and access to resources from the federal government.

STATE RECONSTRUCTION IN ETHIOPIA

The Impact of War

This system has evolved over time, especially in response to crises, the first of which of any note was the outbreak of war with Eritrea in May 1998. Examined in greater detail in the next chapter, this was prompted by the forcible seizure by the Eritreans of a narrow strip of territory administered by Ethiopia as part of Tigray region, which was regarded by the government in Asmara as part of Eritrea. Bonds between the two regimes had been weakening since their joint seizure of power in 1991, and the TPLF leadership in Tigray itself, which largely comprised opponents of Meles Zenawi within the party whom he had exiled back to the region, certainly played a provocative role, but the Eritrean demarche came as a complete shock to the government in Addis Ababa. On the Ethiopian side, the reaction may be ascribed in part to Meles' inability to discipline his TPLF colleagues in Tigray, which formed the core of his own governing coalition, but in very large part also to the sense of nationalist outrage that what was seen as an Eritrean invasion aroused throughout the country.[12] He could not be seen to be giving way to the Eritreans without shattering his support, both in the ruling party and in the country as a whole, and—as leader of a government which was far from having established its right to rule, and was widely regarded as subservient to the regime in Asmara[13]—this left him without room for manoeuvre. Public expressions of Ethiopian outrage at Eritrean seizure of 'their' territory were marked especially by massive public demonstrations in Addis Ababa and elsewhere. It was symptomatic that no senior member of the central government attended the demonstration in Addis Ababa's Maskal Square, at which the most prominent official was the city mayor. Whereas Meles would certainly have preferred to handle the incident diplomatically, a military solution was forced on the regime essentially by public pressure.[14]

In the process, the government became conscious of an underlying sense of Ethiopian nationalism, of which it had previously been unaware. Fighting their own lonely war in an isolated part of the country, and driven to a large extent by a sense of regional identity, the TPLF leadership had come to regard Ethiopia as a cluster of regional or ethnic identities broadly similar to their own. This indeed was the premise on which the system of ethnic federalism had been constructed, with its conception of 'Ethiopia' as a composite construction whose building blocks were the 'nations, nationalities and peoples' of which it was composed. That Ethiopians across the country should be prepared to go to war over a disputed frontier in the regime's own home region of Tigray came as a surprise. The dusty little border town of Badme where the incident that prompted the Eritrean attack took place, previously unknown to the great majority of Ethiopians, became a symbol of national integrity. A reassertion of Ethiopian nationhood, overriding the identities of the individual regions, can be dated to that moment.[15]

The war also called for the recruitment of armed forces on a national basis, vastly expanding a military which, since the demobilisation of the *Derg*'s army in 1991, had rested essentially on the TPLF. This was at least in principle voluntary, though petty criminals were encouraged to sign up by granting them amnesty if they did so. Large numbers of recruits came even from such distant areas as Gambela in the far southwest, and earned themselves a reputation for battlefield brutality that shocked their highland comrades. There was an urgent need for specialist military skills, notably in the air force and artillery, that could only be provided by demobilised *Derg* officers, many of whom were happy to return to what had been their previous livelihood, and in the process to settle scores with the Eritreans. But whereas the previous war had been fought on the basis that Eritrea was an integral part of Ethiopia, this one took on a very

different character. Eritreans, this time round, were not mis-
guided Ethiopians who needed to be incorporated within a single
revolutionary motherland, but foreigners seeking to occupy
sacred Ethiopian territory. Popular reaction to the war helped to
build a nationalism from which Eritrea was excluded.

But while the war served to unite Ethiopians, it also split
Tigrayans. Leading members of the TPLF had long been divided
in their attitudes to the EPLF, resentment towards which dated
back at least to the 1984 famine. Meles Zenawi had, for emi-
nently sensible pragmatic reasons, favoured a collaborative relationship which continued after 1991 and affected issues such as
cross-border trade and Ethiopian use of the Eritrean ports of
Massawa and Assab. He was prepared to take a tolerant approach
to expressions of Eritrean arrogance that derived from the leading role of the EPLF in the struggle against the *Derg*. TPLF
leaders in Tigray tended to take a harder line, partly because they
were in much closer cross-border contact with the Eritreans, but
also because, as already noted, Meles had posted individuals
whom he did not get on with back to Tigray, where he thought
they would make less trouble. When the war eventually ended in
2000 with an Ethiopian victory, gained at a very heavy cost in
lives as a result not least of inept tactics in the early part of the
conflict, he then faced a serious challenge from those within his
own party who felt that his indulgence towards Eritrea had
prompted the outbreak of war in the first place, and that he had
then granted the defeated Eritreans a much more favourable
settlement than the military outcome justified. Ethiopian military sources claim that only Meles' intervention had prevented
them from advancing on Asmara. This split also inevitably drew
on a range of other differences, from factional divisions stretching back to the early years of the struggle, to ideological issues,
resentment at the pre-eminence that Meles had gained in a
movement with a strong egalitarian ethic, and variations in the

viewpoint from Addis Ababa on the one hand and the Tigrayan capital of Mekele on the other. At all events, it says much for the continuing level of internal party democracy that, even after ten years of leading the national government, Meles was by all accounts only just able to cling on to power in the intense debates that took place within the party in 2001. It is equally revealing that while the losing faction were expelled from the party and their positions in government, they were then merely confined to house arrest in Addis Ababa. The reaction to a similar split within the ruling party in Eritrea was to be very different.

Elections, Participation, and the Crisis of 2005

The great majority of African territories experienced, in the late colonial era, a period of intensive political mobilisation—sometimes described as 'the time when politics came'—in which elites seeking to displace the colonial regime organised political parties through which to press their claims, and in the process attempted to build linkages with the mass of the population. Sometimes, a single party was able to express the aspirations of by far the largest part of that population. In other cases, rival parties captured the identities of different sections of it, more often than not on ethnic or regional grounds. But even though these parties were in most states suppressed after independence, and displaced either by imposed single-party systems or military regimes, the underlying political sentiments that they had aroused remained in being, and frequently reasserted themselves in the continent-wide democratic reopening that followed the end of the Cold War.

It is one of the distinctive features of Ethiopia that no such mobilisation took place, leaving a gap in the relationship between ordinary Ethiopians and their government that none of the regimes that have ruled them since then has yet been able to fill. A lower house of parliament elected by popular suffrage was indeed established under the imperial constitution of 1955, but the elections that resulted were contested between individual candidates on a non-party basis, and the institution itself was entirely dismissed by the radicals who sought to displace the imperial regime: these were almost entirely urban, and felt that any rural participation would have served to mobilise established deference to the emperor. When the *Derg* eventually felt secure enough to devise its own constitution in 1984, any representative element was strictly subordinated to the Leninist vanguard party.

The leaders of the EPRDF regime, as already noted, in large part shared the Leninist political assumptions of their predecessors, and had no commitment to multi-party liberal democracies of the kind that, when they came to power in 1991, were being re-established (with varying levels of sustainability) all over the continent. They did however have to position themselves in a global system with which they recognised that they needed to maintain a working relationship, and this in turn entailed at least some acknowledgement of liberal democratic norms. The politics of elections and participation in Ethiopia since that time has turned essentially on the attempt to reconcile such norms, and the new political demands and sentiments aroused by the federalist system, with the primary goal of remaining in power.

Elections on at least a nominally multi-party basis under the constitution of the FDRE have taken place at five-yearly intervals since 1995. The first two federal elections of 1995 and 2000, and the separate elections for the parliaments of the individual regions, took place under the heavy hand of the ruling parties, working with an electoral administration that provided no neutral or impartial arbitration of the process. Despite popular protest especially in the Southern Region, where the democratic promises of the new regime had aroused the greatest optimism, and correspondingly the greatest disappointment, the results were heavily skewed in favour of the regime, and only a small number of opposition candidates were elected. As a study published in 2002 sorrowfully but uncontestably concluded, 'unfortunately, our analyses have demonstrated that the democratic institutions are not allowed to work according to the spirit of democracy'.[16]

By the time of the next federal elections in 2005, events appeared to have moved in the government's favour, and offered the possibility of a vote that would demonstrate genuine and nationwide approval for its policies in a context of open competition. The war against Eritrea had been decisively won. Prime Minister Meles Zenawi had emerged victorious from the internal conflict within the TPLF, and in the process established his supremacy over the political structure as a whole. The regime's economic policies, examined in a later section, had started to achieve demonstrable success, while depending on external linkages—both for aid and for investment—that would be strengthened by an uncontestably democratic domestic political order. Meles consequently felt secure enough to authorise elections in which opposition parties would be free to compete on a reasonably equal footing with those of the government.

The two opposition groupings that emerged to take advantage of this opportunity coalesced around the two alternatives that the EPRDF left open. On the one hand were those, united under the banner of the Coalition for Unity and Democracy (CUD), who were instinctively uneasy about the mobilisation of ethnic identities created by the federal system and the ideas of 'nationality' that underlay it, and sought instead to promote a single countrywide Ethiopian nationalism—an aspiration signalled by the 'Unity' in its title. It also favoured a more liberal or market-oriented system of economic management than the still heavily state-centred approach implemented by the government, and was led by an engineer, Hailu Shawel, with an academic economist, Berhanu Nega. On the other were those who supported the federal structure established by the regime, but complained (with some justice) that this had not been properly implemented, but instead continued to provide an essentially centralised structure of government, under a federalist façade. Under the title of the Union of Ethiopian Democratic Forces (UEDF), this included the Oromo National Congress (ONC), led by an Oromo academic political scientist, Merera Gudina, and the Southern Ethiopia Peoples' Democratic Coalition, led by the Hadiya academic Beyene Petros. As this suggests, the opposition leadership was drawn heavily from an Addis Ababa-centred intellectual elite, albeit one that originated from different parts of the country.

Considerable international pressure was needed both to induce the government to permit the rule changes required to assure the fairness of the election, and to persuade opposition parties to participate. One thing that was not in doubt was the enthusiasm with which voters took part in the process, including large and peaceful demonstrations by both government and opposition supporters in Addis Ababa, and a high level of engagement in the countryside. In this respect, Ethiopia proved to be no different from other parts of Africa. The opposition groupings were able to raise substantial funds, both from the diaspora, especially in the United States, and from donors seeking to level the playing field which would otherwise have been tilted strongly in the government's favour. The opposition was also able to gain media coverage on a par with that of the EPRDF.[17]

The results, when they came in, provided a considerable shock, especially to the government. The CUD won every single parliamentary seat in Addis Ababa, and gained significant support especially in the Amhara region, as well as in the Gurage zone of the Southern region, which supplies a high proportion of Ethiopia's commercial bourgeoisie. The UEDF support was predictably strongest in Oromia and parts of the Southern region, though there were some indications that Muslims tended to vote with the government, possibly because the UEDF leadership was very largely Christian. Exactly how the pattern of support across the country was distributed nonetheless remains uncertain, because when it learnt how the vote was going, the government took control of the election board, and announced subsequent results—largely from the rural areas, where the count was slower—in its own favour. The official tally, which was not announced until nearly three months after polling day, gave 296 seats to the EPRDF, 109 to CUD, and 52 to UEDF, with 13 others. Large public demonstrations against the government were suppressed by force.

At its most basic, therefore, multi-party democracy was aborted in Ethiopia because the EPRDF government was not prepared to tolerate the challenge that it presented to its own tenure. Whether such a system could have been made to work, but for the government intervention, is uncertain but unlikely. The problem did not lie with the voters, who showed the same understanding and enthusiasm for the process as anywhere else in Africa. It would have derived, rather, from the vast policy differences between the parties, ranging from deep hostility to ethnic devolution on the part of the CUD, whose centralist ethos was widely interpreted as a return to Amhara dominance, to the much greater level of devolution sought by the UEDF, in a context in which the politics of compromise was virtually unknown. Nor has Ethiopia yet experienced any government in which the rulers did not ultimately command military force. The most likely if dispiriting scenario must be that even had the EPRDF leadership been prepared to accept the verdict of fair elections, the result would have been a descent into factional squabbling and policy disagreement that would have been resolved before long by military intervention—at the hands of an army in which the TPLF still held the key positions—and the reinstatement of a regime in which it is unlikely that the leadership group who had supported the electoral process would have survived.

Once the government had imposed control, the opposition inevitably fragmented. In a culture that allows little if any scope for legitimate opposition, the tendency of any losing group has almost invariably been to boycott the political process altogether, rather than to engage with it and seek over time to reverse the result, and damaging splits took place over this issue in both of the opposition coalitions. In constituencies where the EPRDF contested opposition victories, the subsequent elections—with official support now unequivocally behind it—went the EPRDF's way, raising its official tally of seats to an overwhelming 327. The same pattern prevailed in regional elections. When the next federal elections were held in 2010, opposition candidates gained only a single seat, while in the 2015 elections, every single seat was won by the EPRDF. A number of reasons can certainly be provided for the failure of the opposition parties, including the internal reorganisation of the EPRDF itself, leading to a far more active presence at the local level; the inability of the opposition, some of whose leaders took refuge abroad, to mount any effort equivalent to that in 2005; and the increasingly evident success of the government's economic development programme. But the bottom line has to be that no legitimate electoral opposition would make any headway against a regime that had clearly demonstrated its determination to cling to power. An Ethiopian regime can, as always, be ousted only by force.

Whatever the role of international pressure in inducing the Ethiopian government to allow reasonably free elections in the first place, and in empowering opposition parties, the diplomatic consequences of the 2005 clampdown were negligible. Already by that date, the monopoly of global leverage enjoyed by the states of Europe and North America in the immediate aftermath of the end of the Cold War was being challenged, notably by the rise of

China, with the result that anything more than token disapproval of the re-imposition of autocracy would have been more likely to result in a loss of diplomatic influence than any significant change of policy within Ethiopia itself. By that time, too, the limitations in Western capacity to impose liberal democratic regimes on African states with unconducive conditions were likewise becoming apparent. But most important of all was the emergence of new threats in the region, notably from radical Islam, that enabled Ethiopia to re-establish its familiar role as a source of stability in a troubled part of the world, destabilisation of which would risk dangerous consequences. As has often been the case in the international politics of the Horn, the domestic regime proved far better able to insulate itself against external pressure than any crude calculation of relative capabilities would have suggested.

Building a Developmental State

There is no government task for which guerrilla warfare provides less preparation than running the economy. During the war itself, economic policy can be little more than a hand-to-mouth task of raising the resources needed to sustain the struggle, both from external sources including supportive foreign states, and from the impoverished local societies in whose territories the war is fought. More important, the attitudes and organisations needed to fight a war are very different indeed from those most appropriate to economic management. Warfare calls for centralised control, directed to the overwhelming priority of military survival and eventually victory, which nothing can be allowed to disrupt. Running a successful economy, on the other hand, requires the encouragement and coordination of multiple different actors—from peasant farmers through to multinational corporations—engaged in different tasks and often pursuing different goals, to which top-down command structures are generally thoroughly unconducive. Added to that, many of the world's most effective insurgent movements, not least in the Horn of Africa, have been guided by Marxist doctrines, and notably Mao Zedong's theory of protracted struggle, which lend themselves to heavily state-centred conceptions of economic management that have proved in practice to be inappropriate to the needs of small developing states within a capitalist world economy.

There was no reason, at the outset, to suppose that the TPLF would do anything but follow the path dependency that guerrilla warfare has characteristically brought to post-liberation development policy. In some of his earliest contacts with outsiders who had penetrated through to the Front's isolated mountain hideouts, Meles Zenawi expressed an admiration for Albania under Enver Hoxha as a model for socialist development. It is unlikely that at that stage he knew very much—or, indeed, anything at all—about Albania, but for anyone looking globally for any comparable experience of a socialist movement cut off from most of the rest of humanity (and opposed to the Soviet Union, which was supporting the *Derg*), there were few alternatives on offer. By the time the TPLF came to power in 1991, at a moment when the state-centred model of development presented by the Soviet Union and its satellites had spectacularly collapsed, Meles had evidently realised that something different would be required. The response provided in the regime's early years was Agricultural Development Led Industrialisation (generally abbreviated to ADLI), a policy which sought to build on the country's agricultural base to create an industrial economy that would add economic value to indigenous raw materials—an approach known in the jargon as 'beneficiation', which had been adopted (usually unsuccessfully) by independent governments in many other African states, especially those with mineral resources. This too looked back to the TPLF's guerrilla experience, in trying to create linkages between the peasantry on whom its victorious strategy had been founded and a modern urban economy, in a way that would bring the benefits of modernity to the most deeply impoverished areas of the countryside.

The problem with this strategy was that the Ethiopian peasantry, especially in zones of desperately poor subsistence farming such as Tigray, simply did not produce a surplus from which ADLI could be generated. There was certainly a 'peace dividend' from the EPDRF takeover, as the militarised structure of the *Derg* regime was rapidly dismantled, peasant conscripts returned to their homes, and friendly relations with the world's most important economies were restored. Meles was identified as one of the 'new African' leaders on whom many of the West's hopes for the post-Cold War development of Africa were pinned, and a welcome surge in aid resulted.[18] But whether the ADLI programme made any significant contribution can be questioned. In addition to its inherent flaws, the leadership at that time was heavily preoccupied first with establishing the new federal structure (which at least in principle devolved development functions in a way that would have severely impeded the implementation of a coherent policy), and subsequently with the war against Eritrea. It was not until after the end of the war in 2000, and the party crisis in 2001, that the regime turned to development as its key political priority.

By that time, Meles' ever-enquiring mind was seeking alternative models.[19] This task became all the more urgent after the 2005 election crisis, which revealed a very worrying weakness in the regime's relations with its population. The answer that he came up with, already prefigured in some of his earlier thinking,[20] drew on the east Asian experience in South Korea, Taiwan, and especially China, and was entitled 'the democratic developmental state'.[21] This sought to integrate Ethiopia into the global economy as a producer of export goods, within an economy in which the state would take a key role in providing basic infrastructure as well as law and order functions, while also encouraging and regulating the private sector, to which was devolved the responsibility for creating the productive base, especially in light manufacturing, on which the success of the enterprise ultimately depended. Central to this in turn was the control of 'rents', an economic term[22] which in Ethiopia came to represent any source of cash that could be captured by the state. It was only by monopolising such rents, which had to be extracted from 'rent-seekers'—identified and demonised as anyone who sought to keep money out of the hands of the state—that the state could gain access to the resources needed to build the essential infrastructural base for development, and to ensure that the 'development' that took place conformed to its objectives. It will already be clear that the 'democratic' element in the developmental state project bore little resemblance to the liberal democracy practised in the West.

This project appears to have been extraordinarily successful, enabling Ethiopia to achieve over some fifteen years a level of economic growth that comes close at least to 10% each year.[23] This has been all the more impressive in that Ethiopia has had none of the windfall profits from high global prices for mineral products (especially oil) that have fuelled equivalent levels of growth in several other African states, and have proved unsustainable once primary produce prices fell. Nor is this a case simply of capital city centred growth. Though Addis Ababa is now a megalopolis of some four million inhabitants, provincial towns have undergone a similar transformation, and way out into the countryside, gangs can be found at work on the roads, and other infrastructural projects. The most spectacular of these projects, the Grand Ethiopian Renaissance Dam (GERD), currently under construction on the Abbai or Blue Nile close to the frontier with Sudan, is projected to generate electricity sufficient to provide power not only for Ethiopia, but for much of the rest of the region. Other dams, principally on the Gibe river in southern Ethiopia, have been designed both for electricity generation and for irrigation. The view from the aircraft window (not the best way to see the Ethiopian countryside, but useful in this case) reveals the replacement of thatch by corrugated iron on the most isolated homesteads. One study shows how a tiny settlement in the Welo area of Amhara state developed over the ten years to 2010 into a small town, with electricity, cell-phones, a greatly improved highway and—not least—changes in the attitudes of the inhabitants themselves.[24] The road network has expanded beyond recognition, accompanied by further investment in railways, and the achievement of Millennium Development Goals in such areas as primary education and the reduction of mother and child mortality indicate that the benefits have extended to the population as a whole.[25] Another very striking example of the public goods provided by economic development is that the drought of 2015/16, which affected a larger part of the country than those of 1974/75 and 1984/85 which established Ethiopia's reputation for famine, was far better managed than previous crises. There were food shortages, certainly, and a drop in the country's economic growth rate; but the creation of an effective monitoring mechanism, coupled with the vast improvement in the distribution network resulting mainly from the road-building programme, made it possible to ensure that the need for relief food was recognised and the food itself provided in time to make all the difference.

In principle, the developmental state offers the possibility of building on Ethiopia's long-established capacity for effective governance in such a way as to transform for the better the lives of its people.[26] A state that works is indeed central to the project, calling for an ability to design and implement plans in a technocratically efficient way. The only other African state to have set about any comparable programme, Rwanda, can likewise draw on a very long tradition of hierarchical authority and centralised rule. This is the point at which the control of 'rents' becomes critical, since these provide the resources needed to drive the public investment on which development depends. In states in which the demands of political maintenance and regime survival require rulers to use all the resources available to meet the demands of the different groups and factions whose acquiescence is essential, nothing will be left to invest. For this reason likewise, competitive multi-party systems in which rival political entrepreneurs compete for popular support are liable to dissipate any resources that might have been used to build a developing economy. It is therefore no surprise that the states that best exemplify the development state model have been essentially authoritarian, at least in the key early stages of the process, even though some of them like South Korea or Taiwan have subsequently evolved into working liberal democracies. In short, this was a project that sought to use the regime's existing strengths in a way that would eventually deliver the 'performance legitimacy' that derived from the benefits that had accrued to the population as a whole.

Running directly counter to the 'Washington consensus' model that equated economic development with the creation of liberal democratic political structures designed to assure the accountability of the rulers to the ruled, the Ethiopian developmental state project might have been expected to attract the hostility of the developed industrial states and international financial institutions whose support (in the form of aid, loans and investment) would be needed to get the project off the ground, not least in a deeply impoverished state which lacked domestic sources of capital and had a large balance of payments deficit. In fact, this did not occur, and Ethiopia was able to draw on high levels of external assistance. To some extent, this was due to the emergence of alternative sources of capital and notably China, which provided funds and expertise for the renovation and expansion of the transport network, especially the key railway link to Djibouti, as well as establishing an industrial park south of Addis Ababa. But in addition, Ethiopia remained a favoured recipient of aid from Western states and institutions, emerging for example as the largest beneficiary of United Kingdom aid worldwide. Even though donors continued in principle to support the mantra that multi-party democracy and effective development went hand-in-hand, at the operational level they were often guided by criteria that emphasised technical efficiency. The administrators of World Bank 'food-for-work' programmes, for example, discovered that Ethiopia actually delivered the public works that they were funding: if the Bank paid for a road construction project, an unannounced check would reveal the building gang at work, on site and on schedule, in a way that all too often was not the case elsewhere.

In practice, the constraints on the development state model have been internal, quite as much as, if not more than, external. In particular, the Ethiopian state, which has been the key enabler of the project on the one hand, has also been a key obstacle on the other. The model required the private sector to assume the leading role in producing the goods needed to drive the export-led growth that it envisaged, and this in turn called for a dynamic and collaborative relationship between state and private sector that a state designed essentially as a control mechanism has been hard put to provide. One problem has been that the state has insisted on retaining control of sectors that would be far more efficiently run by the market, a notable example being telecoms. In a classic example of 'rent-seeking', the state has used its monopoly of telecoms to cream off very large amounts of money that could then be used to fund its infrastructural projects. It may well also have taken the opportunity to monitor traffic for intelligence purposes. As a result, however, the provision of tele-communications services, which have been a key driver of growth in much of Africa, has been less efficient and more expensive than in neighbouring Kenya, or indeed in south-central Somalia where telecoms have worked much better than in Ethiopia, despite having no state at all.

This, however, is a symptom of deeper problems, notably in the promotion of an indigenous private sector of the kind that has been central to development in the east Asian states from which the model derives. The state, and other agencies closely connected to it, have continued to play a significant role in pro-duction, the most prominent example being the Metals and Engineering Corporation (Metek), which derived from the state-owned armaments industry of the *Derg* era, now converted into a general engineering company responsible, for example, for manufacturing much of the rolling stock for the new Addis Ababa light rail system. It remains under the effective control of the military, and provides career opportunities for army officers with engineering skills who have retired from active service. The state-owned Ethiopian Sugar Corporation is responsible for an extremely ambitious sugar development programme in the lower Omo valley close to the frontiers with Kenya and South Sudan, which shows signs of succumbing to many of the problems char-acteristic of large state agricultural projects.[27] Another source of state-managed development has been the commercial enterprises created by different sections of the ruling party, by far the most important of which—corresponding to its dominant role in the EPRDF itself—has been that set up by the TPLF, and known as the Endowment Fund for the Rehabilitation of Tigray, or EFFORT. Formally operating as a private business within a com-petitive economy, this is a conglomerate that includes banking, transport, construction, cement, agro-processing and a range of other activities. It can plausibly be expected to reap considerable economic benefits from its closeness to the government. Equivalent 'party-statals' run by the Amhara and Oromo parties in the ruling coalition have been less influential.

The most prominent company in the Ethiopian private sector is the Midroc corporation, owned by a Saudi businessman, Mohamed al-Amoudi, whose mother is widely believed to have been a Muslim Oromo, and which owns the Sheraton Hotel in Addis Ababa and the Lega Dembi goldmine in the Welega region of western Ethiopia. This has also been close to the regime, though the relationship is a rather more distant one than that of the party endowment funds. Ethiopia, like other African states, has an indigenous business class which (again characteristically) is concentrated in specific groups, notably in this case Muslims and Gurages, a group originating from an area southwest of Addis Ababa, containing both Christians and Muslims, and with a powerful internal ethic of hard work and social solidarity. There is however little sign of the emergence of a dynamic Ethiopian entrepreneurial sector independent of government, and indigenous businessmen are hampered especially by lack of access to capital, which has been ruthlessly extracted from the financial system by the state, in order to fund its own initiatives, and by a pervasive structure of government supervision which—in addition to imposing irksome and time-consuming regulatory constraints—is likewise designed to identify and appropriate profits. The dividing line between 'productive enterprises' on the one hand, and 'rent-seekers' on the other, is an obscure one, and serves to discourage the private sector on which the success of the developmental state depends.

This in turn has obliged the government to look to foreign direct investment more than the expansion of the domestic private sector as the main engine for growth.[28] This investment has derived from a wide range of sources, though with Asian companies—ranging across the continent from Turkey to Japan—to the fore. Floriculture was one of the earliest sectors, with initially Indian and subsequently Dutch engagement, and was particularly well suited to the employment of a large indigenous labour force, mostly women, and to the transfer of expertise to small-scale Ethiopian entrepreneurs.[29] Leather products, notably shoes, are likewise well-adapted to the country's massive livestock resources, and provide a classic example of 'agricultural development led industrialisation'; the industry has been able to recover from the initially devastating impact of Chinese competition by concentrating on areas of comparative advantage,[30] and a Chinese shoe manufacturer has established a factory in Ethiopia. Textiles are another obvious area of interest, attracting investments from Bangladesh, China, India, South Korea and Turkey. Another important source of capital has been the Ethiopian diaspora, now well established in the Gulf, the United States and elsewhere, who are credited with much of the responsibility for the building boom in Addis Ababa and elsewhere, as well as support for small and medium enterprises and for boosting household consumption. Remittances increased by 27.7% a year between 2004/05 and 2012/13, from $US400m to $2,500m.[31]

But despite the regime's recognition of the need for the private sector to assume a dynamic role in expanding the economy, its underlying attitudes remain instinctively statist, and are reinforced by entrenched bureaucratic attitudes that exasperate foreign quite as much as domestic investors. Ethiopia ranks no higher than 132 out of 189 states worldwide in the World Bank's *Ease of Doing Business Index*,[32] though it has risen to 14/47 for sub-Saharan Africa. In the 2016 Global Entrepreneurship Index it ranks only 114 out of 132 states, though again it is slightly above the median for sub-Saharan Africa.[33] Nor, despite its very visible success in promoting general welfare as well as crude indicators of economic growth, has it been able to convert this success into political support. Rapid economic change brings with it disruption that can serve as a source of opposition, and the disproportionate concentration of economic growth in the Oromia region, where the regime's political support has been most fragile, has not brought with it any corresponding political benefits and may well indeed have contributed to dissent.

Managing the Succession

Political succession has been a particularly difficult problem, both for 'Big Man' regimes of the kind that Ethiopia (like many post-independence African states) has been throughout its history, and especially for post-insurgent ones. From the decline of the Gondarine monarchy in Ethiopia in the later eighteenth century, through to the present day, it is difficult to find any unequivocal case of peaceful succession to the highest position in the state,[34] and those of the revolutionary period from 1974 to 1991 were extremely violent, with the ousted leader either killed or (in Mengistu Hailemariam's case) fleeing abroad. Succession in post-insurgent regimes throughout the world has almost invariably depended on 'struggle credentials', or the new leader's role in the conflict that had brought the regime to power in the first place, or occasionally (as in Cuba or North Korea) by dynastic relationship to the former boss. That Meles Zenawi, when he died unexpectedly after a short illness in August 2012, should have been followed by the constitutional succession of the deputy Prime Minister, Hailemariam Desalegn—first as acting Prime Minister, serving out the remainder of Meles' unexpired term, and then from 2015 as full Prime Minister in his own right—is therefore quite exceptional. It was all the more remarkable in that Hailemariam had no struggle credentials of any kind (he had been studying for a postgraduate degree in Finland at the time of the EPRDF victory in May 1991), and that he came from the Welayta people, the second largest group within the Southern Region, which had been incorporated into Ethiopia by force during Menilek's late nineteenth-century conquests. In addition, whereas all previous Ethiopian leaders had been Orthodox Christians, Hailemariam was a Protestant who belonged to the Apostolic Church of Ethiopia, a small sect that was not even among the mainstream churches constituting the Ethiopian Pentecostalist movement. He was thus the ultimate outsider.

It is plausible to suppose that Meles, again unlike the great majority of insurgent leaders who come to power, had been planning for the succession for some time in advance. One key criterion in this respect was that for another Tigrayan or leading TPLF member to take over would reinforce the perception that this was in all material respects a Tigray-based regime, and undermine any claim that it provided equal representation and opportunities for all of the country's nationalities within the federal system. Equally, the selection of an Amhara—as the country's historic ruling group and the one most closely associated with centralised and authoritarian rule—would likewise have undermined the federalist ethos, while the Oromo were both too internally divided and too alienated from the regime to provide a plausible candidate. There is no indication that anyone from the lowland periphery might even have entered the reckoning. There was therefore, if only by default, a strong case for looking for a Southerner, coming from one of the numerous groups who had been admitted to the political mainstream as a consequence of the EPRDF's coalition-building strategy, while also being too small individually to threaten any of the larger ones.

Born in 1965, Hailemariam was too young to have participated in the revolutionary upheavals of the mid-1970s, though his father had been a member of the EPRP, the radical Marxist group most brutally targeted by the *Derg* during the Red Terror of 1976/77.[35] Trained as a civil engineer with a specialisation in hydrology, he became involved in politics as a result of meeting exiled Tigrayans in Scandinavia while working for his postgraduate degree, and subsequently worked his way up within the SEPDM, the Southern region party within the EPRDF coalition. When the regional president was ousted in 2001, for suspected sympathies with the group within the TPLF opposed to Meles Zenawi, Hailemariam took his place, serving for four years before moving to Addis Ababa as an advisor to Meles, before being appointed as deputy Prime Minister and Minister of Foreign Affairs in October 2010. His evident similarity in character to his predecessor—intelligent, quiet, articulate, and (not least by Ethiopian standards) open-minded—doubtless accounts for his designation as deputy Prime Minister at a moment when Meles must have realised that his own days were numbered.

To be designated as Meles' successor was one thing, actually to make good in the job was quite another. In the immediate aftermath of Meles' death, there was evidently much to be said for elevating his deputy, if only as a holding operation while the ruling party—and not least the dominant TPLF element within it—sounded out opinions on the longer term leadership. In this context, the same structural considerations that had led to Hailemariam's appointment as deputy Prime Minister continued to hold good, while his displacement by any of the influential Tigrayans in the government would have risked splits within the TPLF in a way that an outsider did not. The critical moment was when the leaders of the security services, inevitably in some degree rivals, agreed to support him. This in turn reflected Hailemariam's conciliatory style of leadership. No new leader, least of all one from outside the inner core of the TPLF, could expect to exercise anything resembling the level of dominance that Meles had enjoyed after defeating his internal rivals in 2001, and any attempt to do so would have been self-destructive. By leaving the Tigrayan security chiefs in place, and at the same time engaging in greater consultation especially with the three deputy Prime Ministers, Hailemariam has created a more consensual form of government.

This has not been unproblematic. It has necessarily involved slower and more uncertain decision-making, and while the new Prime Minister has evidently had considerable influence over the economic development issues that were his own main area of interest, and has also been prominent in seeking to mediate in regional conflicts, especially in South Sudan, he has had to leave domestic security in the hands of TPLF veterans. A consensual approach is likewise best suited to dealing with routine political issues, but far less capable of reacting to crisis. Ethiopia, like many other African states, has historically tended towards one-man rule, and periods of compromise government, like that of the future Haile Sellassie's regency after the 1916 coup d'état, or the uneasy triumvirate of the earlier years of the *Derg* before Mengistu Haile-Mariam seized complete control, have lasted only until a single leader has established control. And although it is possible that a political process may be developing, this remains to be tested, notably by the challenge of dealing with groups, the Oromo most prominent among them, who have hitherto felt most alienated from the regime.

The Ethiopian Experiment

Twenty-five years after its inauguration, the EPRDF regime has overseen a transformation in Ethiopian political life, the most important element of which has been a dramatic expansion in political space. This has been most evident, not in any significant extension of civil liberties or democratic participation, both of which remain heavily restricted and subject to repressive crackdown when they stray beyond the limits permitted by the regime, but in the proliferation of sites for political activity created especially by the structure of ethnic federalism. Whereas the imperial regime operated within the very narrow framework of the court, and the small elite of individuals associated with it, and the *Derg* within a much larger but still essentially Addis Ababa-based military and intelligentsia, political processes under the EPRDF extend to each of the regional states, and to a range of issues (and notably those created by rapid economic change) that would previously scarcely have figured in the calculus of earlier regimes. The economy itself has undergone a transformation evident throughout the country, and regardless of whether the extremely ambitious aspirations attached to the 'developmental state' are actually achieved, that economy is already far more integrated into national and global markets than was previously the case, as a result especially of the expansion of the communications network.

At the same time, it has become increasingly clear that the political settlement introduced by the EPRDF has failed to resolve—and more than likely *nothing* could resolve—the underlying problems of Ethiopian statehood. It is a truism of political life that the apparently successful resolution of one problem leads to the creation in its place, by an essentially dialectical process, of new problems, or indeed to the re-emergence of the original problem in a different guise. This is very visibly the case with the EPDRF's head-on attempt to deal with the underlying structural inequalities built into the formation of the Ethiopian state, through its programme of ethnic federalism. Bold and adventurous as it was, this provided at least an initial constituency for a new regime drawn disproportionately from a small and distant region of the country, by mobilising the identities of the hitherto excluded peoples of the country, while at the same time retaining some place for those groups who had historically provided the foundations of Ethiopian statehood. Given its origins in Tigray, which in different ways was both a marginal and a central participant in the Ethiopian state, the regime was able to straddle these two constituencies in a way that few if any others could have managed. Indeed, it may well have assumed that its own peculiar position was far more representative of Ethiopia as a whole than was actually the case.

The genie of ethnicity, however, once unleashed, could not be put back in its bottle. The assumption, derived from the TPLF's (and especially Meles Zenawi's) ideological commitment to Marxism, that ethnicity was no more than a superstructural phenomenon derived from economic exploitation, which could in turn be neutralised by representation and development, proved utterly inadequate. Instead, predictably enough, ethnic identities have become increasingly entrenched within a system that had been intended to nullify them. A new politics of identity has emerged, despite (and not least within) a hegemonic party that has become decreasingly able to control the forces of proliferation that it did not create (since these were already implicit in the mismatch between the state and its population), but which it had at least sought to manage. The authority of the central government has perceptibly weakened since Meles' death, and especially in the larger regions, Oromiya and Amhara, party bosses have found themselves looking to their own internal ethnic constituencies, rather than to the centre, not least in order to protect themselves against the ability of the regime's opponents to mobilise those constituencies against them. In the smaller regions, and especially within the highly diverse SNNPR, the system has provided endless opportunities for groups to seek the benefits offered by the federal system to any 'nation, nationality or people' that could make a case for its own separate status. The continuing perception (in a culture much given to conspiracy theories) that the central government was still controlled by and for Tigrayans has given added force to regional identities by directing them against the centre.

The expansion of the political arena has in turn made it necessary to create political mechanisms for resolving differences, in place of the repressive ones that have long provided the basis for Ethiopian governance. This is a particularly difficult task in a state in which open opposition to the ruler has long been equated with treason, political differences have characteristically been managed by byzantine manipulation within the palace walls, and compromise has been regarded as a sign of weakness, which in turn would only encourage further demands, culminating in overt rebellion. This is by no means a uniquely Ethiopian phenomenon. Other historically authoritarian states such as Russia and China suffer from precisely the same difficulty, and have struggled to adjust to a world of open politics in which rival political forces could be publicly acknowledged and the differences between them negotiated to reach some broadly acceptable solution. The hegemonic Leninist party can indeed be regarded as an organisational technology devised to reconcile mass participation with political methods carried over from an earlier era, and it is very much open to question whether the EPRDF is capable of managing the balancing act that it requires.

Further problems arise from the management of the regime's greatest success, in overseeing a level of economic transformation that has dramatically improved the welfare of its population, as measured by indicators such as the 'Millennium Development Goals', and might plausibly have been expected to lead to a corresponding level of political satisfaction and support. Its failure to do so may to some expect be ascribed to the evident falsity of the assumption that economic growth would lead to a reduction in ethnic consciousness. But more than that, rapid economic change necessarily creates its own social imbalances, as different groups (whether defined in regional, ethnic or class terms) benefit (or lose out) to a very different extent, exacerbating the awareness of differences, and intensifying the politics of resentment. That the Oromia region, and especially the area south of Addis Ababa that has long been the primary zone of economic growth in Ethiopia, should have been the main beneficiary of the developmental state, has not reduced the problems of securing political support among the Oromo, but has instead tended to exacerbate them. A classic example of this process was the way in which the Addis Ababa Master Plan, designed as an essentially administrative device to cope with the impact of the city's rapid expansion, aroused high levels of Oromo protest on the grounds that it would involve incorporating 'their' territory into the capital, leading to its cancellation.[36] Issues of this kind are readily convertible into sources of opposition to the EPRDF, and the TPLF in particular. Corruption has likewise become an increasing problem, notably in Oromia, where low levels of legitimacy and accountability combine with opportunities for self-enrichment resulting especially from burgeoning land values.

Over much of the country's recent history, educated Ethiopians have tended to see the country's avoidance of colonial rule as being as much a problem as a benefit. Whatever the pride evinced by the victory over the Italians at Adwa in 1896, or by the heroic efforts of the resistance fighters (commonly called the Patriots) during the Italian occupation between 1936 and 1941, Ethiopia has been regarded as 'missing out' on the benefits brought by colonialism in terms especially of education and economic development.[37] By the later years of emperor Haile Sellassie's reign, the complete contempt of the younger generation of students and their peers for what they regarded as the anachronistic relics of 'feudalism' had reached a pathological level, which could be purged only by an extremely violent revolution, and the period of military dictatorship that followed it. Historic independence likewise brought with it a structural inequality between the 'highland core' on the one hand, and the peripheries, both highland and lowland, on the other, that was independent of the particular form of national government, and in some respects was even more brutally imposed under the *Derg* than it had been under the generally more easy-going (or just less efficient) rule of the emperor.

Since the accession of the EPRDF in 1991, and the attempt at least to fashion a form of government tailor-made to the country's peculiarities, the counterpoint between the perceived advantages and disadvantages of historically independent statehood has become more evenly balanced. Though the old problems of structural inequality are far from having been overcome, especially in the relationships between the agricultural highlands and the pastoralist periphery, there is at least a perceptibly greater sense of common national identity, revealed not least by the reaction to Eritrean attack in 1998, and reinforced by a development process especially in the construction of a countrywide communications network, the value of which has been proved not only by a dramatic rate of economic growth, but by the ability to cope with drought and famine far more effectively than before. That the structure of rule, however strained its pretensions to 'democracy', has been able to promote a level of state-led development beyond the capacities of African states created by the arbitrary whims of colonialism (and consequently obliged to spend much of their resources on 'buying in' the support of diverse groups for the maintenance of the state itself) now looks like much more of a benefit than it once did. At the same time, the absence in Ethiopia of the permitted forms of political mobilisation that emerged in the final years of colonialism elsewhere on the continent continues to impose important constraints on political management.

For the remaining states of the region, the legacies of Ethiopian independence were equally problematic. While all of them experienced formal European colonialism, all of them likewise have had to live beneath the shadow cast by a powerful Ethiopia. On none has this shadow been cast more deeply than on Eritrea.

4

ERITREA

THE TRAGEDY OF THE POST-INSURGENT STATE

The Creation of an Eritrean State

On 24 May 1991, just four days before the EPRDF entered
Addis Ababa, the EPLF marched into Asmara, bringing to an
end a war that had lasted for over a quarter-century, and sealing
the achievement of what had long seemed an impossible dream:
the creation of an independent state in the former Italian colony
of Eritrea, against intense opposition from the largest army in
sub-Saharan Africa, backed first by one and then by the other
superpower. The sense of euphoria at this victory, brought about
at a massive cost in the lives of the combatants on both sides,
lasted for many months or even years afterwards, fostering the
confidence that there was nothing that the discipline, heroism,
inventiveness and organisational capacity manifested in the
struggle could not achieve for the newly independent State of
Eritrea in the years ahead. In Eritrea at that time, I hesitantly
drew the attention of my hosts to the difficulties and disappoint-
ments that other newly independent African states had had to
confront in the period after liberation, but was robustly assured

that in this case my fears were groundless. Eritreans had fought for their independence, I was—rightly—told. They had suffered and all too often died for it. They knew what it was worth, and had the honesty and commitment needed to implement their aspirations for it. They would not waste it. The gulf between those aspirations and the Eritrea that exists after twenty-five years of independence is—in a region not unaccustomed to tragedy—one of the greatest tragedies in the modern history of the Horn of Africa, and any attempt to grapple with the story of independent Eritrea has to start by confronting it. Though leadership certainly had a role—and the difference in this respect between Eritrea and Ethiopia is particularly striking—the more basic answers have to be sought in the quite extraordinary experiences through which Eritrea came to independence, and the ways in which these experiences served not to realise the hopes that the events of May 1991 brought into being, but to negate them.

Many of the difficulties in understanding this part of Africa lie, indeed, in the question of why its peoples *think* in the ways that they do, and in the case of Eritrea this issue is especially acute. War, and especially liberation war, characteristically has a profound impact on the minds of those who have been engaged in it.[1] For many, it gives meaning to the whole of their subsequent existence: it is a period of intense danger, of comradeship, of sacrifice, of unity in the quest for a common and heroic goal, that nothing in later life can equal. For the liberators, it remains a source not only of pride, but of entitlement: that having fought, and been prepared to die, in the great struggle for their country's existence, they have earned the right to a special place in determining its future. The war for the independence of Eritrea was, in this respect, one of the most extreme examples in the history of the world, easily outdistancing other liberation struggles in Africa in the sheer number of years over which it was fought, the intensity of the battles in which its participants were engaged, and the level of sacrifice which it involved, but which at the same time its survivors were able to overcome. It is perfectly understandable that the 'martyrs' should remain at the heart of the Eritrean (or more specifically the EPLF) historic memory. With victory, too, came a sense of the rightness of the struggle, the justification for the decisions and actions that it involved, the legitimacy of the leadership, and the value of the convictions that had led to triumph in the past as a guide and inspiration for the challenges of the future.

Nor did the EPLF have to accommodate any of those strengthening constraints that had limited the EPRDF, but had also ultimately helped it to come to terms with the problems of governing Ethiopia. The EPLF inherited no bureaucracy or set of state institutions. The officials who had staffed the apparatus of Ethiopian rule either fled, or were summarily expelled back to Ethiopia, and in their place, the EPLF, with its fighters and command structure, simply *became* the Eritrean state, operating from behind a desk rather than from a dugout, but bringing with them the same hierarchy and sense of command. Nor did it need—or at any rate feel the need—to build up political institutions that would incorporate into government peoples and communities who had stood outside the liberation struggle. This was a rather more problematic issue than simply building the state, because despite its sense that it embodied a single and united nation, the EPLF and its fighters actually constituted only one part of what now became the people of independent Eritrea. Many Eritreans, until the later part of the war, had—under whatever level of compulsion—remained in that part of the national territory, and especially the major cities, that were controlled by the Ethiopian army. Many more, in this case especially from the lowland pastoralist populations, had fled beyond the boundaries of the state, either to refugee camps or else simply to merge into societies that straddled the artificial frontiers imposed by colonialism. A particularly important group, in terms of their wealth, qualifications, and international contacts, comprised the large diaspora who had spread especially into Europe and North America, and had found work as professionals or businessmen, or indeed in occupations such as taxi drivers, while retaining a deep identity with their homeland, and looking forward to contributing to its future once conditions made it possible for them to do so. Though many of these did indeed return, they found themselves at a disadvantage, and sometimes even the objects of contempt, as against those who had actually fought in the field. Though the EPLF was indeed the state, it was not the nation in quite the same way.

Nor, finally, did the EPLF come to power with any sense that it needed to accommodate other states and actors within the international system. During the liberation war, it had actually benefited from extensive international contacts. The open border that it had maintained with Sudan, and the extensive though covert support of the government in Khartoum, had been enormously important. Eritreans outside the country had been very efficiently organised into a support network for the cause, especially through the regular contribution of financial resources. And though very few states other than Sudan had provided any effective assistance, there was a dedicated set of sympathisers and supporters, especially in western Europe and North America, who had publicised and promoted the case for Eritrean independence. The perception remained, nonetheless, that Eritrea had fought alone, against the hostility of the world, and that it therefore owed no obligations to that world once victory had been achieved. African states, and especially the Organisation of African Unity headquartered in Addis Ababa, were the object of particular contempt, because the founding principles of the organisation, with its insistence on maintaining the territorial integrity of its member states, had been interpreted in such a way as to deny the Eritrean case for independence. When, after Eritrea's formal independence and admission to the OAU in 1993, President Isayas Afewerki first addressed its assembled heads of state, he roundly informed them that the organisation had been a complete waste of time for the previous thirty years. Any outside state, and notably the aid donors who came forward with help for the massive task of postwar reconstruction, that offered advice or sought to influence the policies of the Eritrean government, was treated with truculent rejection—though it must in fairness be remembered that the early 1990s was a period in which Western states were particularly confident not only in their own values, but in their right to seek to impose them on other states, especially in Africa. Few less conducive environments existed for multiparty liberal democracy or a free market economy than post-liberation Eritrea. The effect was however that the new state thus denied itself international support, in a way that was to become particularly damaging after war against Ethiopia broke out in 1998.

The practicalities for securing Eritrea's independence from Ethiopia were unproblematic, given cooperation from the other side of the border. The EPLF constituted itself the Provisional Government of Eritrea, and agreed transitional arrangements with Ethiopia, including continued use of the Ethiopian *birr* as a joint currency, the status of Assab as a free port, with Ethiopian rights of transit also through Massawa, and provisions for trade and communications. Differences over the precise demarcation of the frontier were recognised but left for later resolution. At the risk of failing to resolve issues that might give rise to subsequent problems, these arrangements offered the most plausible framework for healing the wounds that the long years of war had created. On 23–25 April 1993, a referendum was held on Eritrean independence, with the UN and OAU as observers, at which 99.8% of the votes were cast in favour. A four-year transitional government was established, which effectively converted the EPLF into the government: of the 138 members of the National Assembly, the highest legislative authority, 78 were members of the EPLF Central Committee with a further 30 citizens appointed by the EPLF, while the remaining 30 members were elected from provincial assemblies. The President, Isayas Afewerki, combined the posts of Chief Executive and Chairman of the National Assembly. The formal declaration of independence took place on 24 May 1993, two years to the day after the EPLF entry into Asmara. A constitutional commission chaired by a distinguished Eritrean jurist drafted a constitution which was ratified by a constituent assembly in 1997, but remains unimplemented;[2] in principle at least, the transitional arrangements remain in effect, twenty-three years after independence. Nor has the Eritrean government ever published a budget.

Given the quite exceptional circumstances from which the Eritrean state had sprung, it was virtually inevitable that the trajectory of an independent Eritrea would be guided by the ideals and organisation of the struggle, applied to a 'high modernist' conception of national unity and development. There was no question of disbanding the EPLF, once its central objective had been achieved: on the contrary, this was the sole instrument of rule at the government's disposal, and—formally rebranded as the People's Front for Democracy and Justice (PFDJ)—it was retained, though increasingly transformed into a top-down means of control, rather than an army of liberation. The intense conditions under which the struggle had been fought, and the absolute requirements of discipline and obedience that it imposed, in any event made this transformation less evident and abrupt than in nationalist parties elsewhere in Africa that had been created in order to mobilise opinion and win votes in an open and competitive political order. The first to discover the new reality were the soldiers of the EPLF itself, who were informed a few days before independence that they would be required to continue to serve unpaid. This gave rise to a spontaneous protest among those who, having borne the burden of the struggle under the most demanding circumstances, now felt that they had earned the right to an ordinary peaceful existence with their families. It took an uncharacteristically reconciliatory intervention from Isayas Afewerki to persuade them to remain on duty, after which the supposed ringleaders were removed.

Rather than demobilise the army, indeed, the government saw the need to mobilise the rest of the population. Aware that those who had remained under Ethiopian control, and the rapidly increasing number of young Eritreans who had grown up since the struggle ended, could not be relied on to share the solidarity and commitment that the fighters—or *tegadelti*—had acquired in the field, it sought to inculcate the essential values of the struggle through a compulsory programme of national service. Citizens of both sexes between the ages of eighteen and forty were required to undertake six months of military training, followed by a year assigned to some form of development activity, central to which was the training camp at Sawa in the western lowlands which was designed to replicate an isolation from ordinary civilian life comparable to that of the *tegadelti*. There was indeed a huge amount of work needed to reconstruct a society that had been so long at war; the critical point was that this was organised through the same command mechanisms as the war itself. Inevitably, lacking the urgent and obvious imperative of liberation, it failed to generate the same commitment.

The structural reconfiguration of the state followed the same essential logic. One example was the creation of its political and administrative sub-divisions. The old districts (*awraja*) were abolished and replaced by new regions (*zoba*).[3] An analogous process had taken place in Ethiopia, but here it assumed a precisely opposite form. Whereas the Ethiopian regions were redesigned to better reflect the separate identities of the people who lived within them (an aspiration which to the Eritrean government seemed simply crazy), the Eritrean ones were designed to cut across such identities in the name of a homogeneous national identity; so that while the old boundaries broadly corresponded to specific communities, the new ones were intended to bring different groups together. This most evidently involved combining highland and lowland peoples within the same *zoba*, and thus risked the perception that it was intended to bring lowlanders under highland control. Land remained, as under Ethiopian rule, the property of the state, but ancient systems under which its allocation was vested in the local community were abolished in the name of developmental efficiency.[4] Sometimes defined as 'biopolitics', the developmental aspirations of the Eritrean state implied the right and capacity of the governing authorities to reconstruct the conditions of human life itself in such a way as to implement an ideal of what the state and its people should become.[5]

Development politics in the first phase of the EPLF government (1991–98) likewise consisted essentially in concentrating resources in the hands of the state. There was certainly some similarity to the EPRDF regime's hostility to 'rent-seeking' in Ethiopia, but with the important difference that whereas the 'developmental state' in Ethiopia was geared to a long-term vision of integrating the country into the global economy, in Eritrea it was directed to the demands of centralised control. The Red Sea Corporation, originally established during the struggle, became the central government agency concerned especially with the control of imports and exports. Indeed, by offering a premium on the exchange rate set in Addis Ababa, Eritrea was able to garner disproportionate amounts of foreign currency.[6] The currency union with Ethiopia likewise enabled it to buy commodities south of the border which it could then sell on the international market. Like EFFORT in Ethiopia, the Red Sea Corporation became a conglomerate with subsidiaries in such sectors as banking, transport and construction, but facing far less competition than its Ethiopian equivalent. A further vital source of foreign exchange was remittances from the large diaspora, through the maintenance of a system created during the struggle under which Eritreans abroad were required to remit a fixed 2% of their gross income to the government in Asmara. Amounting to a remarkable ability to impose taxation beyond the frontiers of the state, this was enforced by requiring citizens to submit their tax returns in their country of residence to the Eritrean authorities, as a condition for receiving any services from the Eritrean state, such as birth or education certificates; Eritreans resident within the country might also be denied such services, if family members in the diaspora had failed to pay the tax. Remittances provide a critical source of income throughout the Horn, but only in Eritrea has the state been able to control them in this way.

Given that Eritrea benefitted financially from the currency union with Ethiopia, in ways that aroused increasing resentment south of the border, its decision in 1997 to establish its own currency can best be regarded as a largely symbolic assertion of national sovereignty. In what was to be a *leitmotiv* of independent Eritrea, symbolism derived from the struggle took precedence over what in normal circumstances might have been regarded as rational decision-making. Named the *nakfa*, after the town at the centre of the independence struggle, it was assumed in Asmara that this would continue to trade at par with the Ethiopian *birr*, enabling the advantages of the currency union to continue undisturbed. The Ethiopians however refused to permit such an arrangement, insisting that trade between the two countries be conducted in hard currencies, while at the same time introducing new currency notes and demonetising the old ones, in a way that left the Eritrean central bank with a large quantity of now worthless *birr* notes on its hands. Though not the immediate cause of the conflict that was to break out the following year, this was one indicator of the deteriorating relationship between the two former allies that made war possible. It also reflected the fact that whereas on the basis of its internal management, Eritrea might have been able to continue on its own independent path, its increasingly embittered relationships with its neighbours were to prove vastly more damaging.

The 1998–2000 War and its Aftermath

One striking feature of independent Africa has been the ease with which the frontiers established under colonial rule were accepted by the successor states and their peoples. To this generalisation, the Horn remains the great exception, nowhere more viciously contested than in the 1998–2000 war between Eritrea and Ethiopia over the precise location of the boundary between them. Indeed, while the region's other great inter-state war, that between Somalia and Ethiopia in 1977/78, involved the attempted incorporation into Somalia of a vast territory, to which the precise location of the frontier was irrelevant, the war of 1998–2000 was fought over a small strip of contested territory, nowhere more than a few miles wide, and lacking any resources of evident value.

One important contributory factor was the failure to demarcate the frontier on the ground during the colonial period, a failure that resulted from the refusal of the Italian administration in Eritrea to demarcate and thus limit its territorial claims, while at the same time publishing maps that included within Eritrea territory that was administered on the ground by Ethiopia. The records show constant Ethiopian attempts to secure demarcation, equally constantly rebutted on one pretext or another from the Italian side.[7] Formally, at least, this was a clash between two different principles for assigning ownership in the absence of demarcation: according to the maps on the one hand, and to physical possession on the other. This apparently trivial difference, however, could scarcely have resulted in all-out war, save for the mentalities that each side brought to the dispute. One element, already noted, was the importance attached to land in the common culture of the highlanders who controlled the governments of both states. This in turn was greatly intensified by the legacies of the liberation struggle. Both the entire territory of Eritrea in the eyes of the EPLF, and that of Tigray in those of the TPLF south of the border, were endowed with sacred significance as sites of struggle and sacrifice, that could not be abandoned without dishonouring the memory of the martyrs who had died for them. Nor was the Eritrea-Ethiopia border the only area under dispute. Eritrea also engaged in conflicts with Yemen over the ownership of the Hanish Islands in the Red Sea, and with Djibouti over small areas on their common frontier, though these were trivial by comparison with the Ethiopian case.

The immediate flashpoint was the dusty little settlement of Badme, barely worthy of the status of a town, towards the western end of the border, and indeed beyond the territory of the highlanders on either side. Administered by Ethiopia, but shown on the maps as part of Eritrea, this was the place where on 6 May 1998, an altercation between the resident Tigray regional administration and an Eritrean military unit that had entered the area deteriorated to the point at which shots were fired, killing four Eritreans, one of them an EPLF colonel.[8] This ironically occurred at precisely the moment when a meeting of the Border Commission established by the two states to examine the issue was meeting in Addis Ababa. The Eritrean members of the commission returned home and, not long afterwards, the Eritrean army forcibly occupied not only Badme, but the whole strip along the frontier that they held to be part of their own territory. At this point the international community was thoroughly alerted, and efforts were made, notably by a joint mission from the United States and Rwanda, as a regional state that had enjoyed close relations with both sides, to implement a provisional settlement that would make it possible to resolve the issue without recourse to further violence. It seems clear that on neither side did the national leadership intend or expect a war. Meles Zenawi on the Ethiopian side was taken completely by surprise, while in Eritrea Isayas Afewerki appears to have been equally puzzled,[9] though the speed with which Eritrean forces occupied the contested area indicated a level of preparedness entirely lacking on the Ethiopian side. Attempts to broker an agreement broke down over the Ethiopian insistence that the Eritreans withdraw from the occupied territory as a precondition, and the Eritrean refusal to do so. In practical terms, neither leader felt able to back down, without unacceptable damage to his own domestic political standing.

On the Ethiopian side, this intransigence may as already noted be ascribed in part to Meles' inability to discipline his TPLF colleagues in Tigray, which formed the core of his own governing coalition, but in large part also to the sense of nationalist outrage that what was seen as an Eritrean invasion aroused. The equivalent Eritrean refusal to back down is more puzzling, in that Isayas enjoyed a far greater (though, at that time, still not unlimited) level of supremacy in Asmara than did Meles in Addis Ababa, and that war would have pitted Eritrea against an opponent with some twenty times its own population. The answers can, as so often, be appreciated only by reference to the legacies of liberation struggle. The Eritrea-Ethiopia relationship was in large measure regarded in Eritrea as one not between two states, but between two movements, the EPLF and the TPLF, of which the former was by a long way the senior and more powerful. EPLF veterans consistently regarded the TPLF victory in Ethiopia as little more than a by-product of their own struggle in Eritrea, and emphasised the extent to which ostensibly TPLF victories—notably in the critical battle of Shire in February 1989—depended on EPLF engagement.[10] The Eritrean government continued to refer to its Ethiopian counterpart as the *Weyane*, a name derived from the war against the *Derg* that essentially equated the Ethiopian regime with its guerrilla origins. From this point of view, a clash with the TPLF regime in Addis Ababa amounted merely to an elder brother disciplining a younger, a quarrel in which a movement that had defeated the mighty army of the *Derg*, backed though it was by the USSR, need have little fear of losing. Eritreans, too, regarded Ethiopia as little more than an artificial conglomeration of different nationalities that would break apart under pressure into its constituent units. This was indeed a perception that the TPLF in some degree shared, until it was shown to be mistaken by the Ethiopian nationalist reaction to the events of May 1998.

Despite the failure of the mediation efforts, there was then a lull while each side purchased weapons and trained its armies, until intense fighting broke out around Badme in February 1999. The war continued with periods of battle interspersed with fruitless efforts at international mediation, which appear to have been treated by both sides as opportunities to regroup for the next round. Much of the fighting was of the kind associated in Europe with the First World War, with infantry attacks backed by artillery on the trenches occupied by the enemy, with a massive loss of life.[11] Battle deaths can be estimated in the region of 160,000 on both sides.[12] Since the Eritreans were strategically on the defensive, most of the attacks were carried out by the Ethiopians, whose total losses were correspondingly higher, though in relation to population, the Eritrean death toll was proportionately much greater. Eventually, Ethiopian numbers and improved tactical acumen proved decisive, and in May 2000 the Ethiopians achieved a complete breakthrough in the western lowlands towards the Sudanese border, and also recaptured their previous territories in the highlands. Only on the Assab front, separated by a long distance from the fighting elsewhere, were the Eritreans able to hold their own, with a potentially significant effect on the postwar settlement. At this point, Eritrea effectively sued for peace, by agreeing to withdraw from all of the contested areas.

After a war with such a clear military outcome, the resulting political settlement, no matter how one-sided, might well have been expected to be equally definitive. This did not happen, and the agreement that ended the war led to the exacerbation, rather than the resolution, of the differences that had led to it. Sixteen years after the war ended, these differences still remain unresolved. Following talks in Algiers, a ceasefire came into force on 18 June 2000, under which a United Nations peacekeeping force, the UN Mission in Ethiopia and Eritrea (UNMEE), was deployed along a 25-kilometre wide strip between the two armies. This strip fell not merely within Eritrean territory (which was of course disputed), but within Eritrean territory as recognised by Ethiopia, while the Ethiopians established themselves along their own claim line, which has since served as the *de facto* frontier between the two countries. UNMEE was generally effective in maintaining the peace between the former combatants, greatly aided by the facts that it was responsible simply for patrolling a fixed zone, rather than seeking to impose peace over an indeterminate area, and that it was dealing with disciplined armies on either side. It was withdrawn from July 2008 on Eritrean insistence, as a result of the failure to implement the definitive boundary settlement, by which time Ethiopian control of the border zone was secure enough to prevent any major recurrence of hostilities.

The definitive resolution of the issues under dispute was left to two commissions, the Eritrea-Ethiopia Claims Commission (EECC) for public and private claims for loss or injury arising from the conflict, and the Eritrea-Ethiopia Boundary Commission (EEBC) responsible for determining the precise location of the frontier between the two states. Each was set up on precisely the same basis, with two members selected by each state, who then chose a neutral chair, and with very wide latitude over how they conducted their business, while each side committed itself to accept their decisions. It is immediately clear that despite the Ethiopian victory on the battlefield, and the asymmetrical arrangements in Ethiopia's favour for the ceasefire line, the provisions for the ultimate settlement, and notably for the boundary, were to be reached on the basis of complete equality between the parties, thus immediately raising the question of what would happen if the formal arbitration differed significantly from the situation on the ground. It can only be assumed that Meles Zenawi agreed to these provisions in order to reach a settlement that would have to be accepted by Eritrea, and would pave the way for a resumption of normal relations between the two countries, in the confidence that this settlement would be at least broadly in keeping with Ethiopia's goals. This was not to be the case.

The work of the Claims Commission has been widely acclaimed by international lawyers, while having a negligible impact on the actual situation.[13] This took a very broad view of its functions, starting from an assessment of responsibility for the outbreak of war, which it ascribed largely to Eritrea, convicted of having violated international law on the use of force. It went on to examine the conduct of the war in the light of the international law of armed conflict, and concluded with issues relating to violations of international humanitarian law and compensation for damages. Although it made ground-breaking contributions to the role of international law in addressing these issues, its decisions have been almost entirely unimplemented, and neither side has provided the compensation for which it was deemed to be responsible. In the specific context of the Horn, its interest lies largely in the contrast that it provides to the very different approach taken by the Boundary Commission.

This appears, on the evidence of its report,[14] to have approached its task as a limited and technical exercise, concerned to demarcate the boundary on the basis of the written materials available to it, and notably the relevant treaties between Ethiopia and Italy that defined the existence of Eritrea, and the submissions of the contesting parties. It shows no awareness at all of the peculiar and contested history of the border, or indeed of the viciously fought war that had led to the establishment of the commission itself.[15] Strikingly, for example, there was no reference, either in the report itself or in the accompanying maps, to the town of Badme that provided the flashpoint for the war, and the allocation of which to one side or the other was regarded by both as critical. At no point did the commissioners visit the area whose fate they were considering, nor did they take any account of the principle well established in international law since 1919 that the people of an affected area have the right to be consulted over the state to which they wish to belong. This omission was all the more surprising in that the independence of Eritrea had been established through the 1993 referendum in which the people of the territory had voted for or against its independence, a choice that could have been extended to the people of the contested zone; while the 1995 constitution of Ethiopia guarantees to its peoples a right of self-determination up to and including secession, a right that could likewise have been exercised in this case. The original treaties to the meaning of which the commission devoted much of its attention were extremely obscure, unsurprisingly since geographical knowledge and notably maps of the area were thoroughly inadequate at that time. To take one example, the treaties defined the frontier as lying at one point along the lines of the Muna and Belesa rivers. The commission was however unable to find any Muna river in the area that might have corresponded to the treaty line, whereas there were no fewer than three Belesa rivers, any of which might have been the one referred to. This left the commission with a great deal of discretion at its disposal, which—having excluded either self-determination or any reference to information gathered on the ground—left it highly dependent on the documentary evidence, among which maps inevitably assumed a key status, though with no awareness of their deeply problematic provenance. The designation of the UN Cartographer as secretary to the commission may also have enhanced the role of maps as critical documents.

The Boundary Commission demarcation was peculiar in a number of ways. The border town of Zalambesa, for example, was assigned to Ethiopia, but placed in a salient almost entirely surrounded by territory allocated to Eritrea. Further west, the town of Tsorona was assigned to Eritrea, within a semicircular salient jutting into Ethiopia. It is hard to avoid the conclusion that the commissioners, all of whom were distinguished international lawyers, but none of whom had any evident familiarity with the history or cultures of the contesting parties, simply took this to be a largely formal process, implementation of which was guaranteed by the Algiers accords. None of this affected the formal validity of the demarcation, since the commission had been given *carte blanche* to place the boundary wherever it wished, and both parties were committed in advance to accept its findings. The announcement of these findings in April 2002, after a pause during which the Ethiopians had mistakenly supposed that these favoured its position, aroused outrage on the Ethiopian side, especially after the commission had clarified that Badme was placed on the Eritrean side of the border. Since that time, the Ethiopians (while formally accepting the ruling, as the Algiers agreement required them to do) have held their positions on their own claim line, refusing on the basis of one pretext or another to withdraw, or to permit the demarcation on the ground of the frontier designated by the commission, while the Eritreans have demanded its immediate implementation.[16]

In any contest in the Horn between law and power, there could only be one winner. In every respect except the Boundary Commission allocation, Ethiopia enjoyed a position so vastly superior to that of Eritrea that the commission's report has remained unimplemented, except for its publication of a virtual on-line demarcation, complete with virtual boundary markers. Ethiopia was by this time in unquestioned control of the contested area, and had had ample time in which to build up its defences along the frontier that it claimed. It had some twenty times the population of Eritrea, and figured as a major actor in continental diplomacy, while Addis Ababa as headquarters of the African Union and other international organisations had established itself as the diplomatic capital of Africa. The events of 11 September 2001, which occurred while the commission was considering its report, had given the region a renewed strategic importance that it had appeared to lose with the end of the Cold War, and from which Ethiopia (which immediately signed up as a leading partner in the 'global war on terror') was best placed to take advantage. The states which as witnesses of the Algiers Agreements were at least implicitly committed to ensuring their implementation rapidly reneged on their obligations. The result has been that the situation on the ground remains where the ceasefire of June 2000 left it, that the frontier between the two states remains closed, and that Eritrea nurtures an intense and ongoing sense of grievance that reinforces the distrust of the international system that it had inherited from the liberation struggle. Eritrean hostility to the United States remains especially intense.

In Eritrea as in Ethiopia, the war and its outcome shattered the unity of the ruling party, but with much more damaging consequences. The EPLF had never possessed the level of open discussion characteristic of the TPLF, and an early attempt to democratise the movement in 1973, known as the *manqa* crisis, had been suppressed by Isayas Afewerki and his allies.[17] Concerns nonetheless remained over the authoritarian tendencies of the leadership, which surfaced in May 2001 when fifteen leading members of the Front issued an open letter, accusing the government of acting in an illegal manner, and calling on party members and other Eritreans to express their opinion in legal and democratic ways. Including as they did several of the most prominent heroes of the liberation struggle, they evidently assumed that this would give them a degree of protection, and for some four months the dissidents remained at large in Eritrea, helping to prompt a level of open discussion of the country's problems attained neither before nor since. On 18/19 September 2001, in the immediate aftermath of the 9/11 attacks in the United States, eleven of the fifteen were arrested, and have since, if still alive, been held uncharged at an unknown location. Of the remaining four, three were abroad and one recanted,[18] and a crackdown on liberty of expression was reinforced, more intensively than before.

One issue raised by this episode is the extent to which Eritrea's post-independence trajectory can be explained as an outcome of the country's liberation struggle, as against the extent to which it may be ascribed to the leadership, and notably Isayas Afewerki.[19] During the brief opening of 2001, members of the group of fifteen, or G-15 as they were called, expressed views far less rigid than those of the party leader, notably over the need for reconciliation with Ethiopia, despite having shared exactly the same background in the struggle. At the very least, one would have to conclude that Isayas, despite (or because of) his evident skills as an insurgent leader, simply lacked the capacity to make the transition from fighter to ruler of an independent state that was demonstrated to such a striking degree by Meles in Ethiopia. He remained a street fighter, preoccupied with power and survival, and prepared to lash out whenever these were threatened, but lacking any wider vision of the kind that Eritrea desperately needed. With the suppression of the G-15, Eritrea descended into the closed and repressive state that it remained fifteen years later.

Post-War Eritrea: The Traumas of Regime Survival

The war of 1998–2000 had dramatically different impacts on Eritrea and Ethiopia, and marked a parting of the ways in the trajectories of the two countries. Whereas in Ethiopia, Meles Zenawi emerged strengthened both in the ruling party and in the country, and embarked confidently (indeed, overconfidently, as the 2005 election crisis showed) on his programme for economic transformation, Isayas Afewerki in Eritrea was forced back into the struggle mentality that became the all-encompassing *leitmotiv* of state and regime survival. The euphoria of the post-liberation period was abruptly extinguished, along with any plausible agenda for development, and displaced by an overwhelming concern for security, at whatever level. The war, and its aborted resolution, greatly reinforced the sense of threat that had never entirely disappeared, and placed national survival at the centre of the regime's priorities. This in turn was entirely equated with the survival of the EPLF/PFDJ government, threatened not only from without by Ethiopia, but from within through the dissent, readily regarded as treason, of the G-15 and their sympathisers. The securitisation of the Eritrean state reached all the way down to individual Eritreans, faced not only by the extinction of whatever aspirations the end of the liberation war may have given them, but even by a threat to their lives that led many of them to risk the perils of flight rather than remain within the country.

This security imperative was most strikingly indicated by the treatment of the country's youth. After independence, as already noted, a programme of national service was put in place, with the aim most basically of inculcating the spirit of discipline and dedication that had been central to the triumph of the liberation struggle. Until 1998, this followed the eighteen month provision of the original proclamation, and the recruits were demobilised at the end of this period.[20] With the outbreak of war, the demobilised national service men and women were recalled to the army, and the demobilisation of those already serving was halted. After the war ended, however, the survivors' expectation that they would then be released back into civilian life was disappointed, and their service was indefinitely extended. Relaunched in 2002 as the Warsai-Yikaalo Development Campaign (WYDC),[21] recruits were required to remain in service until the age of forty, or in the case of men until fifty. This in turn provided the government with a large conscript labour force, by no means all of which was needed in the army, and many conscripts were therefore allocated to other projects, including not only public works of a developmental kind, but for work on the homes and agricultural estates of senior army officers, and for private companies and notably those owned by the ruling party. Ordinary commercial companies were likewise able to access conscript labour, for whom they paid wages directly to the government, rather than to the individuals themselves. In effect, what had been promoted as a requirement for nation-building and national defence was converted into a system of forced labour, under conditions that met the formal criteria for slavery.[22]

National service or the WYDC can readily be identified as the principal source of refugee flight, which has made Eritrea one of the major refugee-producing states in the world. According to the United Nations High Commission for Refugees (UNHCR), Eritrea—a small state, not at war—ranked seventeenth in the world for the total number of refugees and other 'persons of concern' to the UNHCR among its nationals at the end of

2014.[23] Estimates of the number of Eritrean refugees as a percentage of population placed it eighth in the world, all of the seven states with higher percentages being actively engaged in war or civil conflict.[24] These staggering figures, on top of which allowance must be made for those who died in a vain attempt to find refuge, or who avoided registration, provide the clearest possible indicator of the failure of the Eritrean state to meet the most basic needs of its people.

A state of this kind has no objective beyond the survival of its ruler, and any appraisal of post-war Eritrea correspondingly consists in an examination of how this goal has been sought and—so far—achieved. The first priority must evidently be the sources of power, notably the military, through which the regime maintained its control, and which therefore provided the main threat to the regime itself. This necessarily entailed the degradation of the capacities that the military would require for its ostensible function of protecting the national territory from external attack. Since the Ethiopian army remained entrenched on the country's contested frontier, this involved an element of risk, but in practice the Ethiopians restrained themselves to occasional forays across the border in retaliation for perceived affronts on the Eritrean side, which they have been able to conduct with impunity. There has been no sign of the threat to Eritrea's very existence that has provided the rationale for internal militarisation, and every indication on the Ethiopian side that Eritrea is best left to its own devices. Domestically, the army appears to have been neutralised by stationing it as far as possible from Asmara, while maintaining rivalries between its senior commanders. Overt signs of dissent have largely been confined to the lower ranks, as for example in January 2013, when a group of soldiers seized the information ministry and demanded the removal of Isayas Afewerki, release of political prisoners and implementation of the draft constitution, before being suppressed, though the arrest of a number of senior commanders after this incident suggests that more may have been involved. For the most part, alienated conscripts have taken the exit option represented by flight, rather than seeking to overthrow the regime. Presidential security has reportedly been maintained by Ethiopian opposition groups, who are more dependent on the regime and therefore more reliable than the Eritrean military.[25] Military conscription has itself reduced the danger from urban uprising, by removing a large proportion of the country's urban youth from areas in which they might present a threat. Educated youth, readily identified as a potentially powerful source of political dissent since the student movements against the imperial regime in Ethiopia from the later 1960s onwards, have been subject to especially close control, including enforced evacuation to the most inhospitable parts of the Red Sea lowlands.[26]

The economic basis for regime survival is obscured by a virtually total lack of relevant information.[27] No national budget has been published since independence in 1993, and since estimates of the country's population vary widely, no *per capita* figures can be trusted. Central to the regime's economic model, however—as in Ethiopia, but in very different ways and for very different purposes—is the control of rents, which amount in this case to any source of foreign exchange. This includes the 2% tax on the incomes of Eritreans in the diaspora already noted. It likewise extends to the Red Sea Corporation and its numerous subsidiary companies, which have acquired a virtual monopoly over the domestic economy, especially after investment by Eritreans in the diaspora dried up with the 1998/2000 war. Foreign companies seeking to do business in Eritrea have been required to use government companies for domestic expenditure such as transport and construction, and in the process exposed themselves to the dangers of being indicted for the use of slave labour through the employment of conscripts. The most important of these, the

Canadian mining company Nevsun, maintains a gold, copper and zinc mine at Bisha, some 150 km west of Asmara, in which the Eritrean government also has a 40% stake.[28] Eritrea's recorded exports shot up overnight from $13 million in 2010 to $308 million in 2011, almost entirely in the form of mineral exports to Canada.[29] A number of other mining operations have been negotiated, notably for gold, but to the best of my knowledge are not yet operational. There is in addition a substantial covert economy, run through government nominees and operating especially through Dubai and Qatar, as well as smuggling operations through Sudan that likewise come under government control. One significant exception is people-trafficking, or the payment of bribes to enable escaping refugees to flee the country, which provides a valuable source of income to army officers on the frontier with Sudan.[30]

Ethiopia's diplomatic hegemony has severely restricted Eritrea's international options, not only in Africa but in the global system. The decision by the United Nations, for example, to establish a Commission of Inquiry on Human Rights in Eritrea has to rank as a significant indicator of Ethiopian influence, and of Eritrea's lack of friends who might have obstructed it. So does the imposition of sanctions on Eritrea, prohibiting any trade in arms and also providing for a travel ban and assets freeze.[31] Sheer opportunism, such as Eritrean support for Islamists in Somalia, has undermined the country's diplomatic standing; and having withdrawn from the Intergovernmental Authority on Development (IGAD), the regional organisation headquartered in Djibouti, Eritrea has been unable to gain readmission, and IGAD has come almost entirely under Ethiopian control. Any region with politics as tangled as those of the Horn and the adjoining Arabian peninsula nonetheless provides some opportunities, in the Eritrean case especially across the Red Sea, with the civil war in Yemen as an obvious point of entry. By allying itself with Saudi Arabia and the United Arab Emirates, and allowing its southern port of Assab to be used as a base for operations in Yemen, Eritrea gained both cash and much-needed friends. It has likewise used the refugee crisis as an instrument to secure funds from the European Union. All of this, however, falls within the parameters of a day-to-day survival strategy, rather than forming the basis for any longer-term attempt to tackle the most basic problems of Eritrean governance.

A New Kind of Eritrea?

In appraising the dismal performance of post-independence Eritrea, it is nonetheless important to recognise that the country possesses significant strengths, which it may be possible to mobilise under a different political dispensation. First of all, it has a state that works, albeit in a brutally repressive way, and which is constructed not only on the legacy of the liberation struggle, but on a longstanding tradition of governance, notably in the highlands, that may be expected to endure. It thus provides a classic example of illiberal state-building.[32] This is not a potential Somalia. And however great the abuse of state power, and however entrenched the vested interests of those who wield it, exactly the same was true of the Ethiopian state under the Mengistu regime, which did not prevent that state—however great its continuing problems—from emerging in a substantially changed guise after 1991. There is no plausible scenario for the creation of a liberal and democratic Eritrean political order, and a peaceful succession to the current leadership of the kind that occurred in Ethiopia after the death of Meles Zenawi seems unlikely, but the maintenance of an Eritrean state does not appear to be seriously threatened.

An additional source of strength is a continued commitment to Eritrean nationalism, even among those who have fled the country as refugees and been subjected to the most harrowing experiences in the process. National service does at least appear to have reinforced a sense of national identity between Eritreans from different groups.[33] An idea of Eritrea remains in being, perhaps even reinforced by the tragedies of the post-liberation period, and makes any break-up of Eritrea—let alone any attempted reincorporation into Ethiopia, for which I have been able to detect no significant constituency on either side of the border—improbable. The one major imponderable here is the extent to which identities derived from ethnicity, or especially religion, may have become covertly reinforced within a society in which no legitimate outlet exists through which these can be expressed, but may emerge with additional force once the opportunity to voice them arises. The sense of being Eritrean, nonetheless, appears to be shared by those within the country, and the very large diaspora, which—as a result first of the liberation struggle, and subsequently of post-independence flight—has established an exceptional importance, even in an era in which the transnationalisation or deterritorialisation of African identities has become the norm. The influence of the diaspora was to a large extent marginalised in post-independence Eritrea, as a result of the privileging of the former fighters, but it remains a potentially powerful element in re-establishing linkages, both political and economic, between the country and a global system from which it has almost purposefully alienated itself. Members of the diaspora possess economic resources, skills, and perhaps most important mentalities, which could help to shape an Eritrea significantly different from, and more beneficial to its people than, the regime that emerged from liberation. And while the older diaspora generation—those who fled as a result of the independence war—generally remain committed to the regime, the arrival of a later generation who have fled *from* that regime has greatly expanded the range of debate within the expatriate Eritrean community.

Any project of transformation, however, faces critical difficulties. From an external perspective, the lineaments of such a project are readily defined. First, it would involve the dismantling of the structure of control represented most powerfully by national service, and with it the demilitarisation of a state that has conceived of itself almost entirely in militaristic terms. Second, it would involve an opening of the state to major stakeholders who have been excluded from it, with the diaspora as a particularly important element, but including also significant domestic constituencies such as the intelligentsia, the merchant class, and religious and local community leaders. Third, and vitally, it would require the re-establishment of working relations with Eritrea's neighbours, among whom Ethiopia has a central place. Eritrea since its creation in 1890 has existed effectively as an appendage to Ethiopia, either from an external perspective as a means to gain an entry to Ethiopia through its Red Sea coast, or from an internal Ethiopian one as a zone the control of which has been viewed as central to its own security. In some way, the enduring geopolitical realities of the Horn would need to be reconfigured in a form that served the interests of its varied constituencies, and that would enable Eritrea, in particular, to benefit from the use of its Red Sea ports for trade with the interior, and in the process kickstart its moribund economy by linking it to the dynamic achievements of the Ethiopian developmental state.

Setting out the basic features of a transformed Eritrea is obvious enough. Achieving them is quite another matter. For a start, a 'new' Eritrea would not be founded on a *tabula rasa* of the kind that the victories of the EPLF and TPLF made possible in 1991, when the old regime was simply overthrown in both Asmara and Addis Ababa, and the new rulers were able to create a political structure largely according to their own blueprints. The old truth that the Eritrean state *is* the EPLF remains valid, and a new political order would need to start by co-opting major ele-

137

ments of the old, a task to which leadership would be vital. There is simply no other available organised source of power, save for the possibility of external military intervention, inevitably from Ethiopia, the effect of which can readily be dismissed as catastrophic. Any established power structure, and especially a repressive one, creates interests which are deeply threatened by change, and the removal of which—as the aftermath of the 'Arab spring' all too clearly shows—creates problems of its own. In Eritrea, the key reformist constituency within the EPLF/PFDJ made its move in the aftermath of military defeat in 2001, and was ruthlessly destroyed. Whether any equivalent constituency has been reconstructed—necessarily in the deepest secrecy— within the Eritrean military will become apparent only when the chance of deploying it arises.

Especially difficult is the issue of demilitarisation. A 'new' Eritrea would need to redeploy that very large part of its workforce which has effectively been locked up in the control structure, while at the same time that structure remains central to the way in which the Eritrean state has been managed. From the viewpoint of the country's rulers, it would be necessary to keep its core elements in being, while releasing many of those who have been conscripted into it, whether back to the agrarian or pastoralist livelihoods from which they originally came, or into an urban or market economy that at least at present lacks the capacity to absorb them. From the viewpoint of the conscripts themselves, it raises questions both about their political demands on a state from which they have effectively been excluded, and about the options available for meeting their economic needs. The most obvious outlet would be through further emigration, of a kind that has already presented major challenges both to Eritrea itself, and to the intended destination countries and the states through which emigrants would have to travel.

The reconstruction of Eritrea's external linkages is likewise problematic, depending as it does on a recognition of Eritrea's shrunken place within the regional and global order that sharply contrasts with its self-image as a powerful actor capable of taking on the world and winning, as it did (at least in its own estimation) in the liberation struggle. In recent years, much of the orientation not only of Eritrea's rulers but of a much larger constituency of Eritreans towards the outside world has centred to an extraordinary extent on the issue of the border with Ethiopia. No matter how trivial this all-but-useless strip of territory may be in any broader calculation of the interests and welfare of Eritreans, it has acquired a massive symbolic significance that, thanks to the ineptitude of the Boundary Commission, gives Eritrea legal title to land that has historically formed part of Ethiopia. The abandonment of that title, by a new Eritrean government uncertain of its domestic standing, would necessarily expose it to a charge of subservience to its southern neighbour, no matter what diplomatic formula was devised to sugar the pill. That any Ethiopian government would retreat from its own position on the frontier, which it has maintained over fifteen years at minimal military or diplomatic cost, seems equally improbable.

The issue of the border, however, is itself just one aspect of the way in which the world, and the region in particular, has changed since Eritrea effectively withdrew into self-imposed isolation. During that period, the regional power structure has shifted dramatically in Ethiopia's favour. Part of this shift simply reflects enduring geographical and demographic factors that were obscured by the successful EPLF and TPLF struggle against the *Derg*, and have re-emerged with peace: Ethiopia is just much bigger than Eritrea, and provided that it can remain at peace internally, this difference will inevitably be reflected in regional and global power. Part of it, too, reflects reduced opportunities for leverage that result from changes such as the independence of South Sudan. Instead, the current major fault-lines resulting from the threat posed by radical Islam, even though they provide

Eritrea with tactical opportunities like those presented by the war in Yemen, are more basically deeply threatening to a state whose own population is roughly evenly split between Christianity and Islam. But most critical of all has been the diametrically different trajectories of the two states since their respective liberation movements came to power in May 1991, and especially the sustained level of economic growth achieved in Ethiopia, in contrast to the stasis, at best, in Eritrea. As the bankruptcy of the isolation policy has become increasingly evident, the Eritrean government has begun seeking ways to re-establish a role in the international system. But the world into which Eritrea would need to fit itself, in order to take advantage of the opportunities for peaceful development available to it in the region and elsewhere, contrasts so sharply with its own self-image that adjustment to it would be difficult and even humiliating. The alternative, however, would be what Alex de Waal has termed a 'political-business model' geared only to raising resources sufficient to buy off major rival sources of power within a state in which, as he puts it, 'the trappings of a modern state- and nation-building project ... are wearing very thin'.[34]

5

MANAGING SOMALI STATES

Introduction: The Problems of Somali Governance

The problems of governance in the 'lowland periphery' of the Horn, which in this context corresponds to the Somali-inhabited regions (since the other peoples of the lowland periphery have had no opportunity to establish states of their own) are very different from those in the highland regions of Ethiopia and Eritrea. In the highlands, long-established and culturally embedded structures of hierarchy and authority were manifest not only in the history of state-formation, but also in the formation of guerrilla insurgencies whose own internal effectiveness mirrored that of the societies in which they were forged. One constant factor in the creation of post-insurgent states, both in Africa and elsewhere, is that the internal structure of the movement prior to liberation will be replicated in the character of the government that it is able to create once it has seized power.[1] Disciplined insurgencies in Ethiopia and Eritrea created disciplined states, and the challenge for these was largely one of inducing them to serve the interests of the peoples on whom they were imposed.

141

The Somali experience was the opposite: weakly organised insurgencies, often closely replicating the indigenous social formations and especially clans from which they were formed, had considerable difficulty in transforming themselves into effective governments, even when they succeeded in ousting rivals for power. Throughout the Somali territories, with the perennial exception of Djibouti, the critical challenge has been to create anything that could plausibly be regarded as a state at all.

There have nonetheless been a number of attempts to build states on the fragmentary social base provided by pastoralism, which have achieved very different levels of success. The attempt that has attracted most attention, precisely because its outcomes have generally proved so disastrous, has been in the part of former Italian Somalia, based on the capital of Mogadishu, that is sometimes referred to in the literature simply as 'South Central'. A sharply contrasting pattern has been realised in the former British Somaliland Protectorate, here referred to as 'Somaliland', since its self-proclaimed independence in 1991, the bases for which are explored later in this chapter. The former French Somali Coast, which became independent as Djibouti in 1997, followed a path so different from those not only of the other Somali territories but of the other states of the Horn as a whole, that—save for the region within which it has to exist—it might more plausibly be classed with the states of 'normal' post-colonial Africa. Other forms of administration have emerged in different parts of the Somali lands that do not claim the status of independent states, but which illustrate alternative solutions to the problems of Somali governance. One of these, 'Puntland', comprises an effectively autonomous administration in the extreme north-east of former Italian Somalia (with claims also on part of the territory of Somaliland), which makes no claim to independence. Another, established on a very different basis, is the territory effectively controlled by explicitly Islamist movements, and notably by that known as *al-Shabaab* (or 'the Youth'). To these may be added the Somali Regional State in Ethiopia, often described as the 'Ogaden' (from the name of the principal clan in the area) or in Ethiopian parlance as 'Region 5', which has a very partial level of self-governance under the Ethiopian federal system. This chapter seeks to explore these varying experiments in Somali governance, their failures and at least relative successes, in order to illuminate the possibilities and problems of state formation and maintenance in the lowland periphery of the Horn.

South-Central Somalia: The Contradictions of External State-Building

The rebels who took over the Somali capital of Mogadishu in January 1991 did not inherit a state, as the EPRDF in Addis Ababa were to do four months later. Nor were they in any position to create one, like the EPLF in Asmara. The final vestiges of a Somali state disappeared as its dictator Mohamed Siyad Barre fled from the city in his sole remaining operational tank. Any semblance of a government structure had vanished as the area under the regime's control shrank, and its officials—many of them from the Darood group of clans, marooned in what rapidly became an overwhelmingly Hawiye city—were driven out or sought relative safety in their own clan areas. The rebels themselves had none of the iron discipline of the EPLF, forged over more than two decades of war, but had done little more than occupy the space left vacant by the collapse of the regime. And though they called themselves the United Somali Congress (USC), they represented no more than an *ad hoc* alliance of Hawiye clans that were themselves divided into factions, notably those led by Mohamed Farah Aidid on the one hand, and Ali Mahdi Mohamed on the other.[2] Nor did control of Mogadishu carry with it any authority over the rest of the country. Instead, rival movements with identikit names—the Somali Salvation Democratic Front (SSDF), the Somali National Movement (SNM), the Somali Patriotic Movement (SPM) and others—none of them much more than loose clan alliances, took over their own home territories.

From the viewpoint of ordinary citizens, the 'problem' of not having a state is the absence of the public goods, notably security, that the state is normally expected to provide. They therefore have to seek these goods through the instrumentality of alternative social networks, like those provided by bribery, clan or religion. From the viewpoint of the armed movements, on the other hand, the 'problem' is that winning the war and ousting the dictatorship bequeaths them no mechanism through which they can exercise power and benefit from victory. Building such a structure would require a long and uncertain process of negotiation with other actors, designed to create a consensus under which necessarily limited power would be shared between different stakeholders, leading to the emergence of a reasonably stable order that would in time provide the conditions for enhanced prosperity and a larger product to be shared out between its participants. Such a process took place, as described below, in the former British Somaliland in the north of the country, and to some extent elsewhere, but not in the South-Central zone. The 'warlords', as they were soon called, who controlled the different factional movements, and notably Aidid and Ali Mahdi in Mogadishu, did not have the interest, or probably the capacity, to engage in an exercise of this kind. Instead, they had two alternative mechanisms through which to turn their 'power' into something from which they could benefit.

The first of these was loot, which in the period immediately after the takeover was the only game in town. Coming largely from a pastoralist environment, the fighters who swarmed into Mogadishu had little use for the products associated with urban life, and were concerned only to strip them out and sell them for ready money. Starting with televisions, refrigerators, air-conditioners, generators and other electronic goods, and moving on to copper wire, window frames, corrugated iron sheets and anything else they could lay their hands on, they sold these to merchants from Kenya and elsewhere who descended on Mogadishu to buy them.[3] This in turn massively increased the difficulty and cost of re-establishing governance and ordinary urban life. Other forms of looting likewise targeted the most vulnerable members of society, notably the Digil-Mirifle clans who occupied the Shebele river valley south-west of Mogadishu. These were historically agriculturalists or agro-pastoralists, included significant elements of Bantu rather than Hamitic ethnic stock, and were politically weak and socially despised by Somalis from 'noble' or pastoralist lineages. At the same time, their land was rich, providing resources for commercial farming notably of fruit and vegetables, and made them an obvious target for predation once the structure of order broke down. A third form of loot derived from the famine relief that was delivered in an effort to rescue the starving, and could readily be obstructed and diverted by anyone on the line of supply from the port to the interior.

The second and soon the overwhelming source of benefits was the international system, which emerged as the mainstay of the economy of predation, and has remained so to this day. One of the great gratifications of conflict in Somalia has indeed been the readiness of wealthy foreigners to come up with an ever-flowing stream of resources that have in practice rewarded those who had stolen the goods that were there in the first place. Key to this is the insistence that the world is—and needs to be—divided into 'states', with the result that if any part of it does not appear to have a state, and a government to go with it, it is a matter of the first importance to create one. The first such attempt was a conference in Djibouti in June and July 1991, which was attended by

Ali Mahdi (leader of the less powerful of the two USC factions in Mogadishu), but boycotted by his rival Aidid. This enabled Ali Mahdi to achieve endorsement as interim president, and led to civil war in Mogadishu as Aidid—by this time alerted to the importance of the international factor—rejected the decision. Since that time, an almost endless series of meetings has taken place, most of them outside the country, designed to establish some mechanism that would allow for the creation of something that would count as a national government, and in turn enable its participants to harvest the international resources that formed the critical *raison d'être* for the entire process. The circus proceeded from Djibouti in 1991 to Addis Ababa (March 1993), Sodere, Ethiopia (November 1996), Cairo (December 1997), Arta, Djibouti (April 2000), Eldoret, Kenya (October 2002), Nairobi (January 2004), and Mogadishu (July 2007). The last of these was challenged by a meeting in Asmara, where Eritrea (ever the spoiler in regional politics) sought to establish a rival to the Transitional Federal Government (TFG) which it saw as dominated by Ethiopia. The Arta meeting, which had established the Transitional National Government (TNG) had likewise been challenged by the Somalia Reconciliation and Restoration Council (SRRC), backed by a different set of warlords. As aptly described by Ken Menkhaus, 'the TNG was in essence a piece of paper on a fish hook, thrown into international waters to lure foreign aid which could then be diverted into appropriate pockets'.[4] Much the same could be said of other would-be Somali governments.

It soon became clear that international attempts to create a Somali government would founder without foreign force to back them, and in the process to impose on the indigenous parties some minimal respect for the standards of governance that the donors needed in order to justify their largesse. This introduced a further element of complexity, and meant that intervening states had to stake the lives of their own soldiers, but without changing the basic elements in the process. The first and best-known of these interventions, Operation Restore Hope, was prompted by the 'lame duck' US president, George H.W. Bush, in December 1992, in an attempt to guarantee the delivery of relief food to famine victims, who were being held hostage by the attempts of Somali political factions to control this food in their own interests. Authorised by the United Nations, and led by the United States, this became a key episode in the attempted implementation of a more muscular approach to intervention in the aftermath of the Cold War, built around the belief in a 'responsibility to protect'. After the initial 'shock and awe' as the US army swept ashore and took control of Mogadishu, it soon became clear to local participants that the intervening forces were actors like any other, who could be factored into the calculations of the local factions, and manipulated to the advantage of one side or the other. And although the intervening forces enjoyed a massive apparent superiority in arms and money, they were severely limited by their ignorance of the complexities of the setting in which they were operating, by the constraints on the ability to deploy this superiority that were imposed by global conventions on the use and abuse of force (to which indigenous Somali forces were entirely immune), and by the political setting in their home countries, which in the case of the United States at least excluded any significant number of casualties.

Any optimistic assumption that the intervening forces would benefit from near-universal acclaim for their role in restoring peace and providing food to the starving rapidly vanished in the chaos of Somali politics, not least because their intervention provided benefits to some indigenous actors (and especially those whose relative military weakness led them to welcome outside assistance), while imposing costs on others (especially those who felt that intervention had cheated them of victory). The belief that they could act as a neutral force evaporated, as some factions lined up on their side, and other ones against them, with the result that different groups came to be classified from the intervenors' perspective as 'good guys' on the one hand and 'bad guys' on the other, even though it was often difficult to distinguish between the two. For those who came to support the intervention, being cast in the role of 'good guys' brought immediate benefits, notably through the military force that they could bring to bear, and from preferential access to other resources. The opponents, however, also gained cards that they could play, especially as the defenders of Somali nationalism against foreign invaders (and their traitorous Somali lackeys), and indeed of Islam against foreigners who, initially at least, were largely Christian. In the event, the Aidid faction imposed casualties on the intervening forces that, while trivial in the context of any large-scale military operation, were enough to undercut political support for an intervention which had been conceived, especially in the United States, as a humanitarian operation designed to do 'God's work', as President Bush put it, in bringing food and security to the starving. Over the subsequent decade, until 2005/06, Somali factions were largely left to fight their own battles domestically, while the international community restricted itself to trying to set up some political settlement through the endless and almost entirely fruitless peace conferences already noted. Often described as a period of 'no war, no peace', it started at least to lay the basis for indigenous reactions to crisis.

Given the failure to impose an external structure of control, alternative and potentially much more effective means emerged through which to regulate Somali political space. Central to all of these is the insight that although Somalis have had little sense of or commitment to any specific structure of *government*, they have instead developed highly sophisticated forms of *governance*, through which to maintain some system of order, however fragile, within perennially fractious and divided pastoralist communities. These in turn depend on shared values and principles, broadly characterised as *xeer,* or customary law, which there is strong social pressure to abide by, and through which disputes are managed and contained. Despite the erosion of *xeer,* especially in south-central Somalia, as a result of the conflicts and upheavals of recent years, Somali societies have operated in the absence of formal government institutions in a way that could scarcely be conceived in the agricultural highlands of the Horn, where the breakdown of hierarchical control has been coterminous with violence. Nowhere is this clearer than in the operation of an economy that has functioned with remarkable efficiency despite the lack of overall political control, and has in the process spared many Somalis the levels of destitution that statelessness might have been expected to bring with it.

Somali pastoralist society imposed a need to build and maintain effective social networks over large distances, and these networks were readily adaptable to long-distance trade, in which Somali businessmen have been engaged over many generations. The upheavals resulting from civil war, added to the opportunities presented by the growth of a global economy, led in turn to the formation of a very large Somali diaspora, initially concentrated in ports but dispersed later much more widely, with concentrations in the Gulf, and in parts of Europe and North, as well as in the immediate region. These maintained links with their clan members back home, and have had a massive impact on politics within the territory, something that is explored in more detail later. Their remittances were the most important reason why Somalis were generally able to enjoy a level of economic security well beyond what the extremely limited resources of their homeland could provide. Remittance companies, usually based in the Gulf, developed in order to handle this business, at a low cost and in a highly efficient manner. The enforcement of contracts and maintenance of confidence in the system, essential to large-scale and long-distance money transfers, depends essentially on *xeer*, which imposes responsibilities on kinsmen to guarantee the transactions of their fellow clan members.[5] The creation of a global mobile telecommunications structure was another essential public good, and Somali telecoms companies enjoy a status equivalent to that of the remittance businesses, because the society as a whole is so dependent on them that no one benefits from obstructing them. Other forms of trade, such as that in livestock to the Gulf, operate in the same way. And while remittance and telecoms companies indicate the ability of Somalis to function without a state, these also have interests in political stability that can be deployed to mediate and damp down conflicts that threaten their interests.[6] At the same time, parts of the Somali economy have operated according to the most brutal dictates of force, as with the seizure of lands farmed by the Digil-Mirifle group in the lower Shebelle already referred to, or the role of Kismayu for the control of the ecologically very damaging charcoal trade, fought over by local factions as well as by other actors including the Islamist group *al-Shabaab* and indeed the Kenyan army. Smuggling, the international trade in narcotics, and piracy are among other elements in the Somali economy. It cannot be assumed that trade provides a peaceful and collaborative form of social interaction that contrasts with the violence of the political arena.

A further way of circumventing the inadequacies of the national political process has been through local-level initiatives designed to create political stability through negotiated pacts between the peoples of a particular area. Many of these have been very local and often temporary, but much larger scale arrangements have been put in place both in Somaliland, which merits a section of its own, and in Puntland, in the extreme north-west of Somalia. Whereas Somaliland has explicitly seceded from Somalia, and seeks international recognition as an independent state derived from the British Somaliland Protectorate, Puntland remains an autonomous jurisdiction within Somalia, and derives its identity not from the colonial frontiers but from its association with the Harti group of Darood clans that inhabit the area. It was formed in 1998, like Somaliland several years earlier, as the outcome of a *guurti*, a lengthy meeting of all the interested parties of the region—clan elders, businessmen, intellectuals, and anyone else with the social standing needed to participate—which over several months hammered out the political agreements and compromises required to build authority, in the Somali fashion, from below. Remarkably little material appears to be available about how the Puntland state has actually operated, but it has been able to maintain a leadership succession (despite a war in 2001/2 when its first president, Abdullahi Yusuf, sought and eventually succeeded in gaining a further term in office) that by 2016 extended to five leaders, elected not by popular suffrage but by the regional House of Representatives. Ideally placed for trade with Yemen and the Gulf, it has gained resources both through the diaspora and by exploiting its coastal position—often in illegal ways, through smuggling and piracy. Its leaders regularly participate in Somalia-wide peace processes, and have combined their local base with positions in the various governments established in Mogadishu, giving them some access to the funds provided by international aid, while enabling the region to avoid the external 'peace-keeping' forces that have sought to restrain, while actually enhancing, the insecurity of the rest of Somalia. Along with Somaliland, it provides striking evidence of the Somali capacity to build reasonably effective political mechanisms through processes of local consultation, in the absence of heavy-handed outside involvement.

The third mechanism through which to compensate for the absence of a state, and the most controversial, has been through religion. At one level, this should not be controversial at all.

Virtually all Somalis are Sunni Muslims, and the Sharia and other practices sanctioned through Islam form a constant backdrop to Somali life, adapted where necessary to local practices. Especially at a time of conflict, Islam might well be expected to provide both a moral code and an institutional setting—through the mosques and the Sharia courts—capable of overcoming differences between clans and other factions. It is surprising, indeed, that recourse to religion as a means of dispute resolution did not occur much sooner than was actually the case. An Islamic reaction against the abuse of state power can be traced back to the regime of Siyad Barre, who in 1975 executed a group of Muslim clerics who objected to his imposition of a modernist legal code that in their view ran counter to Sharia (by granting equal rights to women), and a Somali Islamist movement, *al-Itihaad al-Islamiya*, was established through the merger of a number of existing groups in 1983.[7] Several of its members joined the Islamist opposition to the Soviet invasion of Afghanistan, but in the early years after the collapse of the Siyad regime in 1991, it was unable to compete with clan-based insurgencies. Subsequently, as the followings of the various warlords became increasingly fragmented, and were incapable of maintaining the security even of their own clan members, the appeal of Islam increased, aided by hostility to the various 'state-building' efforts of external powers, and the emergence of a much wider Islamist opposition to Western domination most obviously represented by the 9/11 attacks in the United States in 2001. The resulting American intervention in Afghanistan provided an opportunity for a further group of Somali Islamists to gain training in insurgent warfare.

A number of factors then created the basis for an Islamic government in Mogadishu. First, the discredited bands of the competing warlords provided a threat to many and security to none, with no fewer than fourteen factions struggling to survive in the much-looted city. Second, a reviving business community sought protection, not only from these factions but from casual crime. Third, in a setting in which other mechanisms had failed, Islam remained as the sole surviving source of credible social order. In this context, the *kadis* of the various Sharia courts in and around Mogadishu formed a common organisation, the Islamic Courts Union (ICU), which emerged victorious from a war against clan-militias that enabled it to establish control, first over Mogadishu and then over much of southern Somalia. This provided a unified system of justice across the city on the basis of Sharia, with enough support from a variety of broadly Islamist groups to make its judgements stick. The effect was electric, as the militias were driven from the streets, barricades were dismantled, and by mid-2006 for the first time in many years it became possible for unarmed citizens to move peacefully throughout the city. It remains a moment remembered nostalgically by many Somalis.

However, it could not last. In the flush of victory, the ICU leadership, including the element that was later to become much more familiar as *al-Shabaab*, sought to extend their role beyond the city to the whole of southern Somalia, capturing Kismayo in September, as the long-established resident warlord fled. But by turning itself from essentially a city administration into a national movement, the ICU raised questions about its own credentials. Carefully scrutinised, as is invariably the case among Somalis, for its clan base, it was revealed not merely as a Hawiye force (inevitably so, given that Mogadishu is an overwhelmingly Hawiye city), but as having a preponderance at least from one particular sub-clan of the Habr Gedir clan of the Hawiye. In order to maintain its national momentum, it therefore needed to develop a national project, beyond the individual clan allegiances of its components; and the obvious such project, harking back to the early days of Somali independence in the 1960s and to Siyad Barre's disastrous war of 1977/78, was the nationalist one of unity and liberation that set it on a collision course with the ancient enemy, Ethiopia. In addition, it gained legitimacy across the Muslim world, as an authentically Islamist movement that controlled at least the core of a state, and attracted global Islamic fighters like those who had previously sought combat in Afghanistan. Its evident hostility to Ethiopia even induced Eritrea—a state without a shred of sympathy for the Islamist cause, but eager to do anything to destabilise its regional rival— to send EPLF officers to provide military advice. As the unwieldy force rolled towards the frontier, the Ethiopians got their retaliation in first, and destroyed it in a lightning strike in December 2006, sending its disparate elements fleeing to the coast.

At this point, wisdom suggested that the Ethiopians should have stopped, and retreated to the frontier zone. Defeating a ragtag army in the field was one thing, going on to occupy Somalia, and especially a large and hostile city like Mogadishu, was quite another. It was widely asserted that they were urged forward by the United States, in order to consolidate a victory in the 'global war on terror' in which it was then engaged, and to kill or neutralise the contingent of global jihadis who had rallied to the ICU; subsequent evidence indicates, however, that the US strongly advocated against occupying Mogadishu, but that the Ethiopians pressed on regardless, effectively replicating the disaster of Operation Restore Hope some thirteen years earlier, though without either the humanitarian agenda or the local support that the Americans had at least initially enjoyed.[8] This triggered a renewed collapse of governance in Somalia, which was by then showing at least some sign of recovery from the traumas of previous years, and led to further efforts at external state-building.

The Ethiopian occupation, though successful in destroying the threat to Ethiopia's own territory, provoked a return to civil war in which the Islamists, increasingly led by the youth militia *al-Shabaab*, were able to claim the mantle of Somali nationalism against the occupiers and to strengthen their control over much of south-western Somalia, including a substantial presence in Mogadishu. The Ethiopians were able to lower their profile by promoting the formation of an African Union mission, AMISOM, which was established in January 2007 with contributing forces from a number of other east African states, led by Uganda, while themselves withdrawing to areas closer to their own frontier. This set in train a process by which the AMISOM forces sought to control territory on behalf of the internationally established Transitional Federal Government (TFG), which gave way in August 2012 to the Federal Government of Somalia (FGS), officially regarded as the country's first permanent central government since the collapse of the Siyad Barre regime over twenty years earlier. AMISOM proved able to eject *al-Shabaab* from Mogadishu and other major towns, and provide at least some plausibility for an official narrative in which peace was steadily being restored, and national institutions established under the authority of the FGS, including a reconstituted army and police force. The federal arrangement enabled the autonomous government in Puntland to continue undisturbed, and postponed the need to consider the position of Somaliland, which since 1991 had been governed by an independent but globally unrecognised regime.

The viability of this narrative was nonetheless extremely uncertain, its weakness sharply indicated by Transparency International's Corruption Perceptions Index (CPI), which placed Somalia last, 167th out of 167, among all the countries in the world.[9] Corruption at this level cannot be regarded as a 'manageable' issue, ascribable to or containable within indigenous societal norms. It has to be deeply subversive of any kind of moral order. Translated out of the anodyne language of international institutions and aid agencies, what this effectively means is that the African Union and global donors have been providing the FGS with the physical security and the cash resources that enable it to survive without the slightest need for any accountability to the population on whose behalf it was supposedly governing, save for any appearance of consent that could be created by the deployment of the necessary force and money. As a blueprint for the restoration of a Somali government that would eventually be able to restore a legitimate political structure, and to stand on its own once the international scaffolding that supported it was withdrawn, this has to be regarded as highly questionable. A key weakness of the FGS is that its members have been very heavily drawn from foreign passport holding members of the Somali diaspora, many of them drawn back to Mogadishu by the opportunities for self-enrichment that it provided, lacking the levels of integration into domestic society that would be needed to construct enduring linkages with their supposed constituencies, and able at a time of crisis to leave with their accumulated money for their external countries of citizenship.

The overwhelming conclusion of comparative research into the successful restoration of 'failed' states is that this has to be essentially an *internal* process, driven by individuals with a sense of belonging to the societies involved, and with a commitment to recovery that depends, not least, on their own recognition that their futures depend on it. It cannot be created from outside.[10] This conclusion applies with particular force to Somalia, given that the one generalisation about Somali political structures that has stood the test of time is that such structures have to be built up from below, through consensual mechanisms that take account of the disparate interests of all the major players in a highly fragmented social environment. And even though a far greater effort was made in the creation of the FGS than with its predecessors to set up some consultative process for choosing the new government, notably by incorporating federal elements that may or may not stand the test of time, *al-Shabaab* remains better placed than the officially recognised regime to build up its authority from below, by acting as the most visible defender of Somali nationalism and identity against an international attempt to impose political order from above.

The dangers to the population of the contesting and fragmentary systems of authority arising from the conflict between the TNG/FGS and *al-Shabaab* were vividly illustrated by the famine of 2011/12, in which about a quarter of a million Somalis are estimated to have died.[11] Although the drought from which the famine immediately derived was identified in good time, the great majority of the population at risk were in areas then under the control of *al-Shabaab*, which was deeply antipathetic to the international organisations responsible for famine relief, which it viewed as proxies for the regime against which it was fighting. From the viewpoint of these agencies in turn, famine relief operations in *al-Shabaab*-controlled areas carried the risk of sanctions for support to a terrorist group associated with *al-Qaeda*. As is invariably the case with famines in conflict situations, access to food becomes a key means of controlling the populations that need it.

On the other side of the equation, however, *al-Shabaab* and other Islamist movements including the ICU have acted in a way as far removed from any idealised conception of Islam as a pure and uncorrupted expression of the faith, as the FGS has been from equally idealised Western conceptions of statehood.[12] Like any Somali organisation, *al-Shabaab* has had to struggle with the relevance of clan identities, drawing on them at some points to benefit from local support, overriding them at others in the name of Islam or Somali nationalism. Even though much of its pan-Somali appeal derives from its ability to articulate a non-sectarian message, its domestic support has tended to derive from clan groupings excluded from power elsewhere, and especially in recent years from the Digil-Mirifle clans that have been the principal losers from the vicious in-fighting that has resulted from the collapse of the state. *Al-Shabaab* too has had to juggle its domestic priorities against wider allegiances, drawn in this case from the global Islamist movement that provides it with valuable support in some respects, but imposes severe costs in others. Its internal management has often been deeply fractured, both between individuals and between those who see theirs as essentially a Somali struggle, as against those who see it as part of a global *jihad*. In terms of day-to-day relations with the people on whose support it must ultimately depend, it has often also been startlingly inept and repressive, as indicated by its heavy level of responsibility for the death toll in the 2011/12 famine, which had its greatest impact on the people who were under its control, and to whom it had offered the benefits of peace and stability under Islam. It appears to have been every bit as guilty as its civilian political competitors of the ruthless extraction of resources to meet its own priorities. Much of its behaviour, indeed, suggests the mindset of Olson's 'roving bandits', seeking only to extract what they can from the area through which they are moving, rather than 'stationary bandits', who are obliged to manage their resources with an eye to the longer term rather than immediate benefits.[13] At the time of writing, *al-Shabaab* maintains only limited and shifting control over areas outside the main settlements, but has effective information networks throughout much of Somalia. Were it to be obliged to govern any substantive area for any significant time, it would need to develop a sharply changed approach to its local populations, or it would wither and be ousted like the 'warlords' whom it displaced.

Somalia's prospects of re-establishing any form of governance that could plausibly be described as a 'state' have in all probability disappeared. The task of building an effective hierarchy on the fluid and fragmented social base provided by Somali pastoralism was always going to be a difficult task. The state inherited from colonial and trusteeship administration, and briefly boosted by

Somali nationalism, was destroyed by Siyad Barre's self-destructive authoritarianism, and the catastrophic war against Ethiopia. Since that time, periodic attempts by indigenous actors to grope their way towards some reasonably effective means of managing the consequences of state collapse have invariably been undermined by the—generally well-meaning—determination of external actors to come to their aid. The unquestionably idealistic but disastrously counter-productive Operation Restore Hope set in train a pattern of response that has since been replicated. When, in the mid-2000s, a combination of commercial pressures, the moral authority provided by Islam, and local level negotiation offered at least some chance of a workable compromise, this was destroyed by Somalia being sucked into the wider regional politics of radical Islam and the consequent 'global war on terror', exacerbated by misconceived Ethiopian and subsequently Kenyan intervention. The attempt to replicate the mistakes of the past by creating the internationally approved appearance of a state, supported by foreign troops and maintained by foreign money, can only widen the gulf between ordinary Somalis and the mechanisms through which the global system seeks to control them. Whether *al-Shabaab* provides an alternative that would be manageable in domestic Somali terms, quite irrespective of its international acceptability, seems to me doubtful.

Insofar as there is any prospect of managing the problems resulting from a quarter-century of external engagement in Somalia, this can only be achieved by isolation rather than involvement. Given time, and often only at very high cost, Somalis have proved capable of rejecting those proffered solutions that evidently do not work—whether these come from domestic warlords, foreign armies and donors, or Islamist extremists—and gradually feeling their way towards some compromise settlement, usually well short of anything recognisable internationally as a state, that at least meets most of their most basic needs for most of the time. There is no other way of going about it.

The Somaliland Option

The experience since 1991 of the (formerly British) Republic of Somaliland has differed so sharply from that of (formerly Italian) Somalia that it is essential to make clear at the outset that these two cases provide no simple controlled experiment as to what to do, and what not to do, in a Somali setting. To be sure, there are important comparisons to be made between them, just as there are between the two highland states of Ethiopia and Eritrea, but the differences are also critical. Whether the now long-past experience of colonial rule is one of them is open to question, though the President of the Republic of Somaliland displays in his office a set of British Somaliland Protectorate postage stamps, as evidence of the separation of the territory from Somalia to the south. The most that can be said for the British administration is that this was colonialism by neglect, which did as little (and spent as little) as was compatible with the maintenance of social order. In the process, British officials often acquired an enormous affection for the Somali society and mode of life, which they had no desire to disturb.[14]

More important, the dynamics of clan works in a significantly different way in Somaliland from the way it does in south-central Somalia. A single clan-family, the Isaaq, occupy the central areas of the territory, and account for by far the greater part of its population. Though the Isaaq clans, inevitably, are divided both between and within themselves, they provide a reasonably solid ethnic core, that contrasts with the far more mixed and complex composition of southern Somalia, with its two major clan-families, Darood and Hawiye, and the further problems created by the presence of the Digil-Mirifle and other minority groups.

MANAGING SOMALI STATES

Somaliland is by no means entirely Isaaq, with the two Darood clans in the east of the territory, the Dulbahante and Warsangeli, proving particularly difficult to incorporate, while the Gadabursi clan (of the Dir clan-family) occupy its western corner; but its demographic structure means that other clans must either accept Isaaq hegemony and work within it, or else reject the Somaliland state altogether. They cannot expect to control it. At the same time, the fact that the Isaaq clans—characteristically of Somali clan politics—do not form a single united bloc provides other clans with the opportunity to build alliances with one or another group of the Isaaq.

Politically, a sense of Somaliland separateness was reinforced by the formation in 1981 of a northern-based opposition to the Siyad Barre regime, the Somali National Movement (SNM), a name with an evident resonance to the Somali National Party (SNP), the main nationalist movement in Somaliland prior to independence and the union with Somalia. This sought to represent the clans of the former protectorate, not only the Isaaq, though without initially calling for separation from Somalia.[15] Supported by the *Derg* regime in Ethiopia, in retaliation for Siyad's support for Somali opposition movements against the *Derg* within Ethiopia, this was threatened when in 1988, in response to military disasters in Eritrea, Mengistu and Siyad agreed that each would expel opponents of the other from their own territory. Faced by the loss of Ethiopian support, the SNM took the risky option of invading its own home territory, where after initial successes it was subject to vicious repression by the Siyad regime, notably including the systematic bombing of the capital, Hargeisa, and other towns. Many thousands were killed, and looting included the stripping of corrugated iron sheeting for sale in the south, leaving the city roofless. The effect was to alienate Somalilanders not only from the regime but from rule by Mogadishu in any form. The demand for independence from

Mogadishu, especially strong among the refugees in the vast Hartisheik camp in Ethiopia who had been driven from their homeland by the regime, came overwhelmingly from below, and created a reality on the ground that would-be political leaders had to accept.

The grassroots character of the Somaliland political process was central to its success, and accounts in particular for the emergence of local actors capable of negotiating a series of compromise political settlements. Key to this was the marginalisation and eventual dissolution of the armed movement, the SNM, that had led the struggle against the Siyad regime. Elsewhere in the region, the overthrow of the dictatorships in both Mogadishu and Addis Ababa had led either to the seizure of power by the victorious insurgent movement in Ethiopia and Eritrea, or to a vicious conflict between factions of that movement in Somalia. In Somaliland, it worked out very differently, as clan politics subverted both the unity of the SNM itself, and the role of fighters rather than elders and other political negotiators within each of the clans. This was very far from being a straightforward process.[16] On numerous occasions in the years immediately after 1991, fighting broke out—normally between clan-based militias—over issues such as the control of the port of Berbera, which was critical to the livestock trade on which the territory's economy largely depended. On each occasion, a reconciliation conference was called, known generically as a *guurti*, in order to settle the problem. The first, in the town of Sheekh in February 1991, reached an agreement that made it possible to resume livestock exports from Berbera. The second, in Burao a few months later, led to the declaration of independence from Somalia, as a result of a level of popular pressure that it was impossible for the participants to ignore, and to the installation of the SNM chairman, Abdirahman Ahmed Tuur as interim president. This was not enough to prevent further fighting from breaking out in

1992, notably in Burao and Berbera, which had the effect of weakening Tuur's position. It resulted in turn in a four-month meeting in Boroma between January and May 1993, which hammered out the basic structure of the new Somaliland state, and rejected Tuur in favour of the veteran Somaliland politician Mohamed Haji Ibrahim Egal, leader of the SNP in the pre-independence period. The Boroma *guurti* effectively marked the disappearance of the SNM as an actor in Somaliland politics, and the approval of a 'national charter' that became the interim constitution.

The successful creation of a workable political structure in Somaliland rested essentially on three elements. The first was that—in sharp contrast to the experience in Somalia—the process was an internal one, in which external engagement was negligible. It was therefore handled not only in conformity with local norms, but in a setting in which the bargaining power of the principal participants was known and recognised, and was not liable to be upset by the ability of individual actors or factions to call on external sources of force or money that would upset the local balance. The second was that, in a situation in which no participant could exert sufficient force to dominate the others, the political processes of compromise and negotiation displaced military force as the ultimate determinant of the outcome, and the status of armed groups was correspondingly devalued as a source of power. This made possible a successful programme of disarmament, in which fighters were induced to hand in their weapons. The third was the important role of locally-based businessmen in funding the successive peace processes. These had an evident interest in peace, and were initially involved largely in the livestock trade, though they were later supplemented by businesses concerned with telecoms and remittances from the large Somaliland diaspora outside the country. In simple terms, peace was promoted by the benefits of engagement in the global economy, under conditions that insulated the process from external actors with agendas of their own: one candidate for the presidency at the Boroma conference found that his access to Saudi Arabian funds simply did not enable him to buy local support.[17]

The basic political settlement agreed at Boroma has served to carry Somaliland through the subsequent period of over twenty years. To be sure, all Somali political arrangements are in some degree provisional and liable to be challenged, at times forcibly. It was not until 2001 that a constitution was formally agreed, following a referendum, and established a multi-party system in which the number of recognised parties was limited to three—a provision that allowed ample scope for clan-based coalition-building processes. Critically, however, succession to the presidency has on each occasion been peaceful. Tuur handed over to Egal in 1993, and on Egal's death in 2002, his vice-president Dahir Rayale Kahin assumed the presidency. In the first election to be democratically contested after the introduction of the constitution, in 2003, Kahin was re-elected by the narrowest of margins, but the result was accepted by the leader of the losing Kulmiye party, Ahmed Mohamed Silanyo, who in recognising defeat drew attention to the example of Mogadishu as a warning of the dangers of division.[18] Kahin's victory, and its acceptance by the opposition, was all the more remarkable in that he was a Gadabursi, from outside the majority Isaaq clan grouping. He in turn gave way to Silanyo following Kulmiye's overwhelming victory in the next presidential election in June 2010, and Silanyo at the time of writing in 2016 was preparing to step down in favour of another candidate. His willingness to do so may well have resulted from discreet external pressure, and inevitably the prospect of a change of leadership has activated sometimes fraught internal politics. Nonetheless, few African states have been able to manage four successive peaceful handovers.

Somaliland remains a care-and-maintenance state, run with a very limited state apparatus at a level that excludes major initiatives. It possesses neither the funds nor the administrative capacity to engage in any substantial development process, and essentially leaves economic management to the private sector. One key issue is that its sovereignty, despite a quarter-century of independent existence, remains unrecognised by any other state. This is in large part the result of the African Union's requirement that any secession of one part of a member state must be accepted by the government of that state itself, a condition that was met with the separation of Eritrea from Ethiopia and of South Sudan from Sudan, but has not been agreed by any of the fragile administrations in Mogadishu. The African state that would most willingly lead the way, Ethiopia, has been inhibited by its role as the headquarters state of the African Union, and the centrality of remaining at the core of the African consensus to its own wider foreign policy goals. Nor have the post-independence experiences either of Eritrea or (more significantly) of South Sudan provided encouraging precedents for Somaliland in the eyes of the outside world. Somaliland has been able to gain access to some aid, through one mechanism or another, but this has been severely restricted by the non-recognition issue, though any significant increase in aid receipts would undoubtedly undermine accountability and might well give rise to the problems of corruption that have afflicted Somalia. Possibly more damaging is that foreign direct investment is discouraged by the inability of investors to gain insurance coverage as a result of non-recognition, with the result that such investment as has occurred has been very largely in businesses, such as telecoms and remittances, that offer reliable short-term returns.

The most striking indicator of government capacity, and of peace over by far the greater part of the national territory, has been the inability of Islamist movements such as *al-Shabaab* to gain any significant traction in Somaliland, a failure that can most plausibly be attributed to the absence of the level of external engagement that has fostered an Islamist reaction in Somalia. Somaliland proclaims its Islamic identity through the prominent display of the *shahada*—'there is no god but God, and Mohamed is his prophet'—on its flag, and there is certainly a significant Salafist element within Somaliland Islam, but Islamist infiltrators from further south have been readily picked out in a society in which every person's identity, notably in clan and sub-clan terms, is instantly recognised. There has nonetheless been a very visible shift towards a much stricter interpretation of Islam, evident especially in women's clothing. Whereas Somali women were accustomed to dress in the most vivid colours, and very few of them were veiled, they are now more often clad in order to be inconspicuous, and full veils are increasingly common.

The main threat to Somaliland comes, however, not from Islamist movements but from the overlap on its eastern frontier between its own territorial claims and those of the Puntland administration that formally remains within Somalia. It is central to the Somaliland claim to independence that it is the successor state to the former British protectorate, and that it is therefore entitled to the sovereignty that it briefly exercised in June 1960, under the African Union principle binding members to accept the colonial frontiers inherited at independence. This extends Somaliland jurisdiction over the members of the Dhulbahante and Warsangeli clans who inhabit the eastern parts of its territory. The quasi-state of Puntland, on the other hand, claims to represent and administer the territory of the Harti clan grouping, which includes the Dhulbahante and Warsangeli, and rejects former colonial boundaries as an illegitimate division of its people. To the extent that each administration rigidly insists on its own jurisdiction, conflict between them is inevitable. In practice, the peoples of the disputed area adapt to the demands that this division imposes on them in a characteristically pragmatic way.[19] In sharp contrast to the territorially defined communities of highland Ethiopia and Eritrea, to whom boundaries are sacred and between whom apparently trivial differences could trigger a vicious war, for Somalis these are merely ignored, unless they create opportunities for bargaining and manipulation, depending on the advantages to be gained from association with either side.

After a quarter-century of *de* facto independence, most Somalilanders have no memory of a united Somalia, and there is no evident interest in reunion with the south. The Somaliland experience demonstrates the possibilities and limitations of statehood within the constraints of a pastoralist society. Such a state necessarily rests on a process of accommodation between different groups and interests that is open to constant contestation and occasional conflict as bargaining opportunities change, and actors shift from one alliance to another in a kaleidoscope of varying patterns. An enduring hierarchy of control is impossible to maintain, and where conflict occurs, this is not in an attempt to impose such a hierarchy, but rather a demonstration of capacity in order to assert a bargaining strength that the actor concerned believes to be undervalued. The power of the state itself, or of the coalition that currently controls it, is always open to question, and almost invariably falls short of the 'sovereignty' defined by international convention, and expected by external actors. Its ability to achieve transformational change, of the kind sought for example by the Ethiopian 'developmental state' is virtually non-existent, and such long-term change as does occur is the result of adjustment to external circumstances, such as the emergence of global trading opportunities or new technologies like mobile telephony of which Somalis are characteristically very quick to take advantage. Within these limitations, however, it provides a means to achieve at least a measure of welfare for most of its people, in a way that the attempt to impose more rigid forms of governance has signally failed to do.

A further peculiar experience of Somali governance that deserves at least a comment is that of the Somali-inhabited region of Ethiopia, which under the 1995 Ethiopian constitution formally enjoys the status of an autonomous region, entitled to self-government including the right of secession, which would in principle allow it to become part of a united Somali state. In practice, 'Region 5' (as it is often known in Ethiopian parlance) from an Ethiopian perspective provides a vital buffer zone between the rest of the country and the threat of instability and Islamic terrorism emanating from Somalia, and is subject to a heavy Ethiopian security presence. The Ethiopian government nonetheless still needs to find some means to manage the internal politics of the region, not so much for constitutional reasons as to limit the threat that it poses. The starting point for this process derives, inevitably, from its clan structure, which resembles that of Somaliland rather more than that of Somalia, in that a single clan, the Ogaden clan of the Darood clan-family, holds a potentially hegemonic place in the region that is in some ways analogous to that of the Isaaq in Somaliland. Ogadenis probably account for rather less than half of the region's population, but the remainder is split between all of the Somali clan-families—Darood, Dir, Hawiye, Isaaq and even a few Digil-Mirifle—and the Ogadenis are both centrally placed and constitute a majority in most of the region's seven zones. In internal terms, a political settlement in the region therefore calls for the support (or at least acquiescence) of a substantial element of the Ogaden clan; the alternative, of trying to put together a coalition of the other clans against the Ogaden, is in practice too complex to be manageable. The Ogadenis, however, have had their own movement, the Ogaden National Liberation Front (ONLF), formed in 1984, which claims to represent all Ethiopian Somalis, but is widely regarded within the region as the voice of the Ogaden clan.

The ONLF joined the transitional government formed by the EPRDF after its takeover in 1991, and initially controlled the regional government.[20] Like the OLF, however, it was pushed out as a result of the EPRDF's refusal to accept independent partners not under its own control, and displaced by the central government approved Ethiopian Somali Democratic League (ESDL), effectively a coalition of the minority clans against the Ogaden. After a series of splits, the ONLF resorted to armed conflict, its most prominent action being an attack in April 2007 on a Chinese oil exploration camp in the region, which resulted in the deaths of nine Chinese and about sixty-five Ethiopians.[21] Predictably, this was followed by a major security clampdown, leaving the Ethiopian government as far as ever from managing its perennially fractious Somali population. Remarkably, none-theless, it succeeded in finding an Ogadeni, Abdi Mohamed Omar (known as Abdi Iley, the one-eyed),[22] who both com-manded a following in his own clan and was prepared to work with the Ethiopian state. After taking over as regional president in 2010, Abdi Iley forged a relationship with the Tigrayan com-mander of the Ethiopian army in the region, and to build up his own paramilitary force, the Liyu Police,[23] which recruited many of its members from former ONLF fighters, and acquired a repu-tation as his personal force, not only within the Somali region but across the frontier into Somalia. So effective was this combi-nation that the ONLF was (at least temporarily) neutralised, and the Ethiopian national intelligence service was excluded from the region. In the process, the Somali region of Ethiopia, centrally placed in relation to the Somali people as a whole, has emerged as a significant autonomous actor in wider Somali politics, pro-jecting Ethiopian power while also in some degree acting inde-pendently from the central Ethiopian government. This is a significant reversal of the 'normal' situation, in which the region has been subject to the competing forces of central Ethiopian government on the one hand, and nationalist movements orches-trated from the Somali Republic on the other.

All Somali political arrangements are temporary and subject to upheaval, and the future of this one is uncertain. Nor is there any independent evidence as to the level of support that it actually commands among Ethiopian Somalis, or of the quality of governance that it has been able to deliver—both highly contested issues. It does however illustrate both the possibility of combining a credible external force (and in this respect, the Ethiopian army commands much greater respect than the multinational AMISOM force in South Central Somalia) with some level of local engagement, and also the amount of latitude that the central Ethiopian government has been prepared to allow to a local boss who abides by the essential criterion of obedience to the dominant political order.

The Djibouti Anomaly

This book has as yet left virtually unmentioned the fifth and smallest state in the Horn, the Republic of Djibouti, that appears at least to stand outside both the fraught and unstable politics of the region, and the conceptual framework that the book has sought to apply. In fact, Djibouti is very closely integrated into the region, and provides a peculiar and revealing slant on the way in which it works. Located close to the centre of a circle whose circumference encompasses the most northerly point of Eritrea, easterly and southerly points of Somalia, and westerly point of Ethiopia, its late nineteenth-century origins as a distinct territory mimic those of Eritrea, both as a port on a trade route made newly important by the opening of the Suez Canal, and as an entry point for Ethiopia. Initially called the Côte Française des Somalis, its name was changed to the Territoire Française des Afars at des Issas in 1967, and to Djibouti (after its capital and major town) at independence in 1977. As the second of these names indicates, its population consists largely of Issa Somalis (from the Dir clan family), comprising close to two-thirds of the total, who extend into Ethiopia and Somaliland, and Afar, who also inhabit neighbouring parts of Ethiopia and Eritrea. Djibouti's at least relative detachment from the politics of the region enables it to serve as the headquarters of the Inter-Governmental Authority on Development (IGAD), an organisation whose anodyne name (the only one among African regional bodies that fails even to mention the region concerned) accurately reflects its very limited influence.[24]

Central to Djibouti's role in the region is the fact that its French colonisers, unlike the Italians in Eritrea, had no interest in using it as a launch pad for conquering Ethiopia. They sought instead to use it, far more constructively, as a coastal entrepôt from which to trade into the interior, a function expressed notably by the railway from Djibouti to Addis Ababa completed in 1916, and with the partial exception of the Eritrean ports of Massawa and Assab between 1952 and 1998, it has since provided Ethiopia's major outlet to the sea. With the closure of the Eritrean ports after the outbreak of the Eritrean-Ethiopian war in 1998, it has become Ethiopia's absolutely critical lifeline. More basically, the fact that its *raison d'être* was essentially commercial rather than territorial has helped to insulate it from the conflicts that have afflicted the region.

Three further factors account for its quite exceptional level of stability. First and most obvious has been the French security guarantee, which continued after independence (which took place at precisely the time of the Somali-Ethiopian war of 1977/78), and has been assured not only by treaty but by the continuous presence of French troops on the ground. This in turn has been relatively easy to maintain, because Djibouti has not been under any significant threat of attack. By far its most important neighbour has been Ethiopia, whose own security depended on maintaining its stability, and (unlike the Ethiopian attitude towards Eritrea) has never pressed any claim to incorporate it into its own territory. Although Djibouti accounted for one of the five points of the star on the Somali flag, which stood for the five territories (with Somalia, Somaliland, and the Somali-inhabited regions of Ethiopia and Kenya) that Somali nationalists sought to unite into a single state, it was at the far extremity of the Somali-inhabited lands, and no attempt to take it over could have succeeded without first achieving the massive task of defeating Ethiopia. In terms of Somali clan politics, Djibouti provided the Issa clan with a state of their own, and gave them no incentive to participate in a united Somali state that would inevitably be dominated by the larger groupings. Djibouti's third neighbour, Eritrea, has only a short (but disputed) frontier at the far edge of its own territory, and even though this led in 1996 to the military confrontation characteristic of Eritrea's relations with all of its neighbours, it did not threaten the stability of Djibouti as a whole.

Second, as a city state, in which the capital accounts for over 70% of the country's total population, Djibouti has a demographic structure very different from that of the rest of the lowland periphery. There is no pastoralist population in a position to engulf the capital, as happened in Mogadishu in 1991, or could likewise occur in Somaliland in the case of a breakdown in the political pact that maintains stability there. The minority Afar people, who provide the greatest potential threat, live largely on the northern side of the Gulf of Tajura that bisects the country, and although Djibouti city on the southern coast has a large Afar population, it is clearly under Issa control. And finally, Djibouti exists beneath the shadow of its giant neighbour, Ethiopia, whose interests in the port are so great that any upheaval that endangered the *entrepôt* would incite Ethiopian intervention, which in itself provides a major deterrent.

This security has in turn enabled Djibouti to survive as a thoroughly neo-patrimonial little state under the control of a family oligarchy. The government since independence has remained under the control of the Mamassan sub-clan of the Issa, and in nearly forty years has been led by only two men, the first president Hassan Gouled Aptidon, and then from 1999 his nephew Ismail Omar Guelleh. These have had to ensure that they did not alienate any of the major stakeholders on whom the country's stability ultimately depended, and notably the Ethiopians, the French, and the major Issa clan factions, but this has been a relatively straightforward task, aided by the revenues accruing from the port, and by the aid opportunities or political rents deriving from Djibouti's strategic situation.

The group most evidently excluded from the political process have been the Afar. In principle, an Issa-Afar power sharing deal underpinned politics at independence, with an Afar prime minister ostensibly balancing an Issa President. In practice Afars were systematically side-lined. Under the banner of the Front for the Restoration of Unity and Democracy (FRUD) the Afar launched an insurgency in November 1991 and overran much of the northern and Afar-inhabited part of the country. After a demonstration in the Afar quarter of Djibouti city had been brutally suppressed in the following month, this was largely confined to the Afar home region which was in any event so undeveloped and marginalised that it made little difference to the rest of the country. A substantially enlarged Djibouti army with French support regained control over the region, and under a peace agreement in 1996, a number of FRUD members were brought into the government, which essentially resolved the problem by buying the support of Afar leaders.

The basic stability assured by French and Ethiopian support has in turn enabled the Djibouti government—subject to the limitations in its freedom of action that this imposed—to extend its own contacts, and the rents that it could gain from them, profiting from the strategic situation that became as significant in the early twenty-first century as it had been when the territory was first established in the late nineteenth. A management agreement for the port with Dubai Ports World was greeted at first with some misgivings by the Ethiopians, but has generally worked effectively, and provided capital for the substantial expansion called for by the rapid level of economic growth in Ethiopia, linked to an upgrade of the line of rail to Addis Ababa opened in 2016, which has reinforced Djibouti's monopoly over Ethiopia's external trade. At the same time, congestion at Djibouti port has intensified the Ethiopian search for alternative outlets, including a projected port development near Berbera in Somaliland. More spectacularly, the regional instability prompted by Islamist insurgencies both in the Horn and in the Arabian peninsula, and the breakdown of order in Somalia, have provided windfall opportunities for a state that provides a perfectly situated location for external forces seeking to monitor and control the region. Following the 9/11 attacks, the United States in November 2002 took over the French base in Djibouti, Camp Lemonnier, the sole US military base in sub-Saharan Africa and home of the Combined Joint Task Force—Horn of Africa (CJTF-HOA) of the US Africa Command, assuring further external support at the same time as a rent of $60m a year.[25] It provides surveillance and drone facilities against both *al-Shabaab* in Somalia and the Islamist forces in the Yemen civil war. Djibouti was likewise well placed as a base for the operations of the multi-national naval forces established to counter piracy in the Gulf of Aden and the Indian Ocean, which resulted from state breakdown in Somalia and operated largely from ports in Puntland. It also hosts the only Chinese base in Africa, and Japan's only overseas base anywhere in the world.

In short, Djibouti is deeply engaged in the problematic politics of the Horn, but has so far managed to arbitrage the resulting conflicts to its own advantage. It is subject like the other states of the region to the overwhelming presence of Ethiopia, but has managed Ethiopian hegemony in a way that supports rather than threatening its domestic political order. Its port has enabled Ethiopia in particular to evade the consequences of Eritrean hostility and the closure to it of the Eritrean ports of Assab and Massawa. It has benefited from the instability resulting from state breakdown and Islamist insurgency. It appears at least to enjoy the best of all possible worlds. Its problem—as yet only latent but potentially highly threatening—is that in gaining these advantages, it has become an obvious target for forces of regional instability, most prominently Islamist in character, that may engage in attacks on Djibouti city, which has a large excluded population open to mobilisation. Any credible threat to Djibouti would deal a major blow to the structures of order maintained within the region by Ethiopia and externally by a large coalition of leading global powers. Stability in such a contested part of the world must inevitably come at a price.

6

THE HORN, THE CONTINENT
AND THE WORLD

Structures of Regional Hegemony and Contestation

It will already be abundantly clear that the states of the Horn are deeply affected by their relationships with one another, and that these relationships in turn are very heavily influenced by the internal social structures, patterns of domination, political systems and indeed governmentalities of the states themselves. As in the rest of sub-Saharan Africa, the process of state creation itself involved an at best only very partially successful attempt to impose the imperatives of statehood on ecological zones and indigenous societies that in large measure failed to correspond to the political units into which they were squeezed by the assumption that statehood was a necessary constituent of global order. Where the Horn differed from the rest of the continent was in the specific form that this process took, and the nature of the subjection that it involved.

It is likewise evident that this process was intensely problematic, and that while a significant level of conflict could plausibly be expected, simply as a result of the way in which the geogra-

phies of the Horn brought very different peoples into close association with one another, the pattern of late nineteenth-century
territorial partition greatly exacerbated the difficulties. One measure of this is that the basic principles governing relationships
between African states after their independence from colonial
rule, enshrined in the Charter of the Organisation of African
Unity agreed—significantly, in Addis Ababa—in 1963, and
extended in that of the African Union in 2000, failed to secure
the level of consensus in the Horn that they elsewhere enjoyed
among almost all of the continent's independent states. On the
face of it, these principles, which sought to establish the sovereignty of African states by insisting on the recognition of the
boundaries of these states at the moment of their independence,
and on non-intervention in the internal affairs of other states,
appeared to assure an equal status to all of them, which in turn
would help to ensure stable and peaceful relationships between
them. This has indeed generally been the case, and looking back
over the period of more than half a century since the OAU's
creation, the decisions taken by its founding fathers at that
moment can be hailed as a far-sighted and generally extraordinarily successful attempt to establish the diplomatic structure of
independent Africa. From the viewpoint of the Horn, on the
other hand, the creation of the OAU and the principles that it
established looked like an effective imposition of Ethiopian
hegemony. These principles themselves were bitterly contested at
the founding summit by the Prime Minister of the Somali
Republic, since they denied the right of all Somalis to choose the
structure of statehood under which they wished to be governed.
They likewise negated the right of Eritreans to self-determination, a right that was later established only as the result of a long
and extremely costly war. Even within the Somali Republic, they
prevented—and continue to prevent—the people of Somaliland
from enjoying the recognised independent statehood that has

been internally validated by an overwhelming popular vote in favour of independence. The distinctiveness of the Horn is emphasised by the fact that it is only there, and in neighbouring Sudan, that secessionist movements have succeeded.

Ethiopian hegemony, indeed, represents the central problem in the regional dynamics of the Horn, while potentially at least providing a mechanism for assuring the region's stability. For so long as a single state at the heart of the region has a population vastly greater than that of its other states combined, together with an effective government, an economy likewise far more important than those of its neighbours, a powerful military, and alliances both in the continent and beyond it, that state is necessarily the critical element on which the structure of regional relations depends. Only at two moments in recent history has its role appeared to be threatened. The first was at the time of the revolution immediately after 1974, when the collapse of the imperial regime and widespread disorder throughout its territory prompted the government of the Somali Republic to launch its ill-fated invasion. In the event, as was the case with the post-revolutionary attacks on France after 1789 and Russia after 1917, revolution and invasion greatly strengthened the state, and enabled it to defeat its enemies both foreign and domestic. The second was in 1991, when Eritrean independence, and the introduction of a constitution that—at least ostensibly—offered all of Ethiopia's peoples a right of self-determination extending to secession, provided a roadmap for a post-Soviet style break-up into a collection of successor states. Despite the threats to Ethiopia's internal stability represented especially by the regime's difficulties in providing a stable and acceptable role for the Oromo, that possibility has likewise receded—aided as in 1977 by the external challenge that came in this case from Eritrea in 1998. Any framework for regional order must consequently take the dominant position of Ethiopia as a given.

THE HORN OF AFRICA

Historically, and in a comparative perspective, the presence of a large and powerful state at the centre of a region has been every bit as likely to prove a destabilising element as a stabilising one. Such states, like the United States in the Americas, imperial and Soviet Russia in central Europe and Asia, or China in East Asia, readily acquire a hegemonic or even imperialist attitude towards their neighbours that arouses intense resentment. Ethiopia provides indeed a classic case of such attitudes. An empire not merely in name but in behaviour, it has assumed a sense of manifest destiny towards its region that was most visible in its expansion under Menilek, and that—even though its boundaries, save for the acquisition and then loss of Eritrea, have been constant for over a century—lives on in the memory of its neighbours. In its own self-image, such neighbours have been a source of threat, from the time of Ahmed Gragn in the early sixteenth century through the colonial epoch to the fascist invasion of 1935, and indeed the Eritrean attack of 1998. In that of other regional states, the threat comes from the opposite direction.

Nor has there been much in the recent experience of the peripheral states of the region to diminish the common perception of the Horn as a deeply unstable part of the world. The evident failure of post-independence Eritrea has left a state whose current trajectory is unsustainable, and whose resentments over the aborted boundary settlement have prevented any resolution of the wider issues that underlay the war of 1998–2000. Though I am inclined to discount the danger that the problems of the Isayas regime might culminate in state breakdown of the kind seen in Somalia and South Sudan, and there is always a chance that a successor government might seek to end the truculent isolationism that has characterised the country since 2000, there is nonetheless a threat of serious instability on Ethiopia's northern frontier. In Somalia and South Sudan, Ethiopia's neighbours include the two most definitively collapsed states in the modern world, with little prospect that either can re-establish any viable form of domestic political order at any time in the immediate future. External intervention especially in Somalia has exacerbated its problems, and in the process extended the resulting conflicts into Kenya, which at one stage appeared to have managed its ethnic Somali populations far more successfully than had Ethiopia. The emergence of radical Islam as a significant political force in much of the Horn has reduced the scope for compromise settlements, given that—at least in the hands of its most vocal exponents—this is an absolutist ideology that rejects any form of governance that these regard as contrary to the will of God. The prospects for reducing the threat posed by Salafism lie largely in the capacity of its leaders to alienate their own popular base, coupled with measures to improve the quality of governance among the affected populations, and reduce the resentments—one of which is that promoted by external intervention—that have led people to look to alternative forms of rule. As Alex de Waal's relentless exposure of the cynicism and corruption of the region's ruling elites trenchantly demonstrates, there is little reason to envisage enlightened political leadership as a potential solution to the problems of bad government and consequent instability.[1]

Under these circumstances, it may well seem to be straining optimism to suggest any scenario that might enable the region to escape its dismal legacies of conflict. Yet there are at least some elements that, potentially at least, offer prospects for improvement. One of these is the independence of both Eritrea and South Sudan, which—regardless of the post-independence trajectories of both states—has at least resolved longstanding civil wars in both Ethiopia and Sudan. In the process, the governments both in Khartoum and in Addis Ababa have lost the sources of leverage that encouraged each of them to seek to destabilise the other. In South Sudan, as in south-central Somalia, regional states in collaboration with other international actors have for the most part sought to resolve the problems that resulted in state collapse, and even though their efforts have generally been unproductive and indeed even counter-productive, they have an any rate been preferable to deliberate attempts to foment the conflicts by providing diplomatic and military support to one side or the other. A second major improvement has been the disappearance with the end of the Cold War of the incentives that these conflicts gave to each of the superpowers to support its own regional proxies in opposition to those of its rival, notably through the provision (especially by the Soviet Union) of vast quantities of weaponry. Instead, global powers like regional ones have generally been concerned to resolve conflicts rather than exacerbate them. In particular, China as the new significant actor in global politics has been concerned (outside East Asia) to promote peaceful settlements, as the best way to ensure the reliable delivery of the raw materials that constitute its own most important reason for engagement in Africa. The global collaboration in opposition to Somali piracy follows a similar logic.

One key element in the new politics of regional conflict management has been support for peacekeeping forces, both in Somalia and Sudan. In Somalia, as already noted, such forces have proved extremely problematic, and as likely to promote conflict as to resolve it. In the two Sudans, they have been rather more beneficial, though without being able to create the basis for any lasting settlement to the conflict in South Sudan. Ethiopia's principal contribution has been to provide the vast majority of peacekeepers patrolling the Abyei frontier zone between Sudan and South Sudan, where its disciplined and efficient armed forces appear to have done a very competent job. Much more noteworthy, however, is that both states should have been willing to accept Ethiopia—until very recently a major element in destabilising Sudan—in this role, and the evidence that this provides of Ethiopia's contribution to the establishment of regional security structures. There is none-theless a sharp discrepancy between Ethiopia's now evident desire to promote stability in its borderlands and its actual ability to do so. Conflict in both Somalia and South Sudan derives most evidently from the difficulty of creating states under extremely unpropitious conditions, but Ethiopian relations with the Somali states and, especially, Eritrea are undermined by a very long history of resentment that any attempt to create regional peace on Ethiopian terms must inevitably exacerbate.[2]

Any more deep-seated process of regional conflict management and resolution must derive from some transformation of regional relationships, rather than just the removal of salient sources of conflict. In this context, the Ethiopian developmental state offers at least the possibility of creating a framework for a greatly increased level of regional cooperation. For a start, Ethiopia's own development can only be encouraged by stability within and between its neighbours, and give it every incentive to help to resolve rather than foment conflicts elsewhere in the region. This must account in large part for its collaboration with other regional states and the international system as a whole in efforts to create settlements in both Somalia and South Sudan, however ineffectual these have been. It has tacitly supported the government in Somaliland, which offers a potential alternative outlet to the sea to both Djibouti and the Eritrean ports, without stepping out of line from the AU consensus that so far impedes formal recognition. With its most problematic neighbour, Eritrea, it has generally maintained a wait-and-see policy, holding the existing (and, of course, disputed) frontier, but without overt intervention in internal Eritrean affairs, presumably in the hope that a future Eritrean regime will opt for more consensual relations.

Further regional integration can only depend on the extension to neighbouring states of the benefits of participation in the Ethiopian development process, and in this respect the state that has most to gain, Eritrea, is also the one most determined to resist incorporation into a necessarily Ethiopian-dominated developmental partnership. It would take an epic shift in Eritrean governmental attitudes to prompt a reorientation from national security to public welfare as a driver of the country's domestic policies as well as its external priorities, and if any such shift is on the mental agendas of potential successors to the Isayas regime, the complete prohibition on expressing any opposition to that regime within Eritrea prevents it from leaking out. Potentially, however, it would immediately unblock the ports of Massawa and Assab, enabling these to share (and compete) with Djibouti as beneficiaries of the rapid expansion in Ethiopia's external trade, and restore the cross-border linkages with northern Ethiopia that were brought to an instant halt by the outbreak of war in 1998.

The Ethiopian government's own projects for regional integration rest heavily on the Grand Ethiopian Renaissance Dam (GERD), which has been conceived as a source of abundant electricity not only for Ethiopia itself, but for its neighbours and especially the two Sudans. Indeed, given the GERD's closeness to the Sudanese frontier, and its location in an inaccessible part of the Blue Nile or Abbay gorge, it would probably be more straightforward to extend its powerlines into Sudan than into Ethiopia itself. The Nile waters have since the earliest times been a source both of linkage and of potential conflict between the upstream states—of which Ethiopia is in hydrological terms by far the most important—and the downstream states of Sudan and notably Egypt.[3] Any possible disruption to their flow has correspondingly aroused an intense reaction as an existential threat not only to the Egyptian state but to Egyptian society as a whole, and the initial Ethiopian diversion of the waters in preparation for building the GERD in 2013 aroused a demand on the Morsi government then in power that Egypt should launch a military attack. Since then, the potential benefits of the project have come to the fore. Hydrologically, it makes sense to store the water upstream, where both the higher altitude and the greater depth-to-surface ratio of a dam in the gorge result in a lower evaporation loss than in the Merowe and Aswan dams in Sudan and Egypt, both of which are relatively shallow and in areas of intense heat and aridity. Both Sudan and Egypt stand to gain access to cheap electricity, provided by Ethiopia essentially as the diplomatic price for acceptability. And the costs of disruption to the downstream states—on a worst-case scenario unleashing a devastating flood down the entire Nile valley—would be catastrophic. Equally, the project represents a significant shift in diplomatic power from Sudan and Egypt, both affected by major problems of domestic stability, to Ethiopia.

Big dams have served throughout the world—from the Hoover Dam in the United States to the Three Gorges Dam in China, and in Africa including the Aswan High Dam on the Nile and the Kariba and Cahora Bassa dams on the Zambezi—as classic 'high modernist' projects, loudly trumpeting human control over the environment, while often leading to very damaging side effects and failing to deliver the massive benefits that they have promised. The GERD, as the epitome of the Ethiopian developmental state, is just such a project, and whether it will actually provide abundant cheap electricity without causing disastrous environmental damage remains to be seen. Since the GERD has no irrigation component, it will not (save for evaporation) remove water from the downstream states, but it is likely to take many years to fill, since only in years of high Ethiopian rainfall will it be possible to retain much water without damaging downstream consumers, and there are doubts over whether it will actually be able to generate the megawatts claimed for it. Analogous claims were made, but have not been delivered, for the Merowe Dam in Sudan.[4] Other grand projects in Ethiopia, notably for agricultural development in the country's southern and western lowlands, have lagged, while also raising issues over the impact on the indigenous peoples of the regions involved.[5] At the very least, however, the GERD provides a narrative for development and integration in a region in which these have been few and far between.

A second great regional development initiative, the Lamu Port, South Sudan and Ethiopia Transport Corridor (LAPSSET), is altogether more speculative. A vast infrastructure project, this is designed to provide road, rail and pipeline linkages from a new port close to the ancient trading city of Lamu on the Kenyan Indian Ocean coast through to Juba in South Sudan, with a further link into southern Ethiopia and eventually to Addis Ababa.[6] Once achieved, this would transform the transport economies of South Sudan and southern Ethiopia, and provide an alternative to Djibouti that the congested Kenyan port of Mombasa is ill-equipped to do, tying these economies into the East African and Indian Ocean networks and orienting them away from their historic links to the Red Sea. It nonetheless faces critical problems, not only in raising the capital and in the engineering feats required, but in the extremely uncertain political environments both in South Sudan and in the Somali-inhabited parts of Kenya through which the corridor would have to pass. The lead time would likewise be considerable.

The key to stability in the Horn rests, as always, with Ethiopia. In a region with such massive internal power disparities, hegemonic stability is the only kind on offer, and this requires at a minimum that Ethiopia remains reasonably stable internally, and that it is capable of articulating a wider regional project that promises mutual benefits rather than the prospect of mere domination to its neighbours. For so long as these requirements hold, continuing instability in the peripheral states breaks down into a set of problems that can be managed separately from one another—if at all. It is striking, indeed, how *little* Ethiopia's own development trajectory has been affected by the traumas of its three most problematic neighbours, Eritrea, south-central Somalia, and South Sudan. Each of these, moreover, is quite distinct from the other two, and raises challenges of different kinds that—if they can be resolved at all—can be handled separately from one another. A settlement in South Sudan does not depend to any significant extent on one in Eritrea, nor either of these on peace in Somalia. On an optimistic scenario, a process of regional stabilisation could proceed piecemeal from one to another, as opportunity offered. The Horn nonetheless provides ample evidence that optimistic scenarios, like those greeting Eritrean independence in 1991 or South Sudanese independence in 2011, have almost invariably been confounded.

Continental and Global Agendas

The place to consider the impact of the wider international system on the regional politics of the Horn is—where this book puts it—at the end. That impact has certainly been important, and at times critical, but both its direction and its effect has depended, and continues to depend, on the way in which it responds to the internal structure of the region. For those who view the world in global terms, the massive power disparities between the most developed states on earth, and a part of the world notorious for its abject poverty and internal conflicts, are so gross that it seems axiomatic to assume that one is in a position to control the other. For those within the region, likewise, who seek to account for its often manifest failures, it is comforting to view its inhabitants as the victims of external exploitation and aggression, and thus to deny agency to its rulers, rather than regarding these as being to a significant extent the authors of their own misfortunes—an approach that equally denies them credit for any initiative that may have turned out well.

For a striking refutation of these assumptions, one need only look to the experience of both Ethiopia and Eritrea in the immediate aftermath of the seizure of power by the EPRDF and EPLF in May 1991. Both states were at that moment deeply impoverished, traumatised and degraded by many years of warfare, internally divided, and in desperate need of whatever support they could find. A clearer case for their dependency on the international system could scarcely be envisaged. Yet in each case—though certainly more successfully in one than in the other—their responses to the crises of state reconstruction and recovery were orchestrated and imposed by the leaders of the incoming regimes, who confronted would-be outside advisers and aid donors with firmly articulated domestic priorities to which these had to adapt. The same was true of the Rwanda Patriotic Front leadership in the aftermath of the genocide in 1994. Leaders, of course, have to take account of the situations in which they find themselves, domestically every bit as much as internationally, and a failure to read these correctly is likely to result in disaster, but they nonetheless have a significant level of initiative in the way that they choose to go about it.

The distinctive feature of the Horn has been that Ethiopia has almost invariably served as the prism through which outside powers have viewed the region, providing a source of understandable discontent or even outrage to other actors. Ethiopian regimes have characteristically been in a position to present the 'stability' of their own country, and of the region as a whole, as requiring external actors to pursue policies that broadly corresponded to Ethiopian interests, even in cases where those interests were to have disastrous long-term consequences. In the case of the federation of Eritrea with Ethiopia in 1952, for example, the imperial regime then in power was able to link its claims on Eritrea to the global security structure that the United States was seeking to build in the context of the Cold War, by offering the

US a vital communications base in Eritrea. When the Soviet Union then sought to establish its own presence in the region, in the aftermath of its ejection from Egypt by Sadat, this required it to align with the weaker of the two regional states, Somalia, because of the alliance that the United States had already established with Ethiopia. When, following the 1974 revolution, Ethiopia sought to change sides, the USSR was happy to switch alliances, leaving the United States facing a dilemma as to whether to switch in turn to the Somalis—an option that it declined to take, preferring to stand aside in the expectation that Ethiopia would eventually once more become available. The new global power in the region, China, has likewise placed its interests in Ethiopia ahead of any others. The African consensus, as already noted, has consistently favoured Ethiopia, both over the Eritrean issue and over the claims of Somalia on the Somali-inhabited zone that the Ethiopian government had annexed in the course of the colonial partition.

These patterns have been replicated since 1991. In the aftermath of the Cold War, when issues of superpower alliance ceased to be relevant, the then dominant Western powers looked to liberal democracy, 'good governance', conflict resolution and economic development as a linked package of measures designed to bring Africa into the 'Washington consensus' through which a new and universally beneficial global order was to be created. Ironically, the only regime in the region that implemented any genuine system of multiparty democracy, validated by a peaceful transfer of power as the result of an election, was also the only one, Somaliland, that has consistently been denied international recognition. Only very partially did the region's leading state, Ethiopia, conform to this agenda. It scored highly on good governance and conflict resolution, but paid only the most formal lip service to the demands of multi-party democracy, and pursued economic development through policies derived largely from the

East Asian experience that openly derided the Western liberal model. The EPRDF regime under Meles Zenawi nonetheless achieved the status of one of the 'new African' governments that were deemed to lead the way to the reformation of the continent, while Meles himself acquired little less than a heroic role, both within Africa and beyond it, as an articulate spokesman for continental aspirations—a role indicated by his position on the British government's Commission for Africa, and as African representative on the climate change agenda. This position was then strengthened by the collapse of government in Somalia, which enhanced Ethiopia's importance as a source of regional stability, and by the events of 9/11 and the 'global war on terror'. Though the Ethiopian government has carefully worked in tandem with major external powers over regional issues, it has never subordinated its own interests to those of others.

The most striking example of Ethiopia's capacity to control the terms of external engagement in the Horn remains its ability to disregard the findings of the Eritrea-Ethiopia Boundary Commission in the aftermath of the 1998–2000 war. However flawed these findings may have been, the two parties committed themselves in advance to accept them, and at least implicitly, the witnesses to the Algiers Agreement that established the boundary and claims commissions—including the United Nations, the United States, the African Union, and the European Union—were committed to guaranteeing their implementation. Quite simply, this has never happened, and Ethiopia's external relations have in no way suffered as a result. At the root of the Boundary Commission's failure, nonetheless, lay its inability to engage (or simply lack of interest in engaging) with the distinctive cultures and complex politics of the Horn.

Exactly the same problems, though in a very different setting, underlay the still more damaging failure of external actors to secure any effective solution to the collapse of the state in

Somalia. Again, the almost automatic reaction was to seek to apply a package of measures derived from global assumptions about the proper management of the international system. The difference was that, whereas in the case of the Eritrea-Ethiopia boundary, there was at least a power structure in place through which to impose a solution (however much this outraged the Eritreans and disregarded the legal formalities), no such power structure existed in Somalia. Nor could one be created, either by the incursion of foreign military forces, or by the endless and evidently futile attempts to introduce some 'state-building' formula that merely induced different groups of Somali politicians to go through the motions of setting up the appearance of a government that, depending on external force and external money, could never be expected to establish any effective system of governance once the scaffolding that supported it had been removed. The conclusion has to be that this is a part of Africa that marches to its own drum, and to which no solution to its manifest problems is likely to be effective that fails to take account of its own peculiar dynamics.

The most evident of the global changes now affecting the Horn, the rise of Asian states and especially China, can be fitted without much difficulty into the existing pattern of regional relationships. However spectacular its incursion onto the regional scene, China is an external state like any other, not significantly different from—and in some ways not even equal to—the European colonial states and Cold War superpowers that have historically figured as the major external actors in the Horn. It lacks the territorial ambitions of the European colonisers, and despite the role of the Chinese model as a guide for the Ethiopian developmental state, it does not provide the source of ideological inspiration that the Soviet Union exercised from the later 1960s through to the late 1980s, notably through its remarkable impact on the Ethiopian revolution. Its strategic interests, despite the newly established base in Djibouti, do not remotely approach those of the USA and USSR, and it conforms to historical norms in focusing its attention on Ethiopia, as the diplomatically dominant state of the region, as well as the one most propitious for economic investment. This investment, especially in infrastructure but also in some manufacturing facilities, has helped to strengthen the basis for Ethiopian hegemony.

A potentially far more disruptive shift is the startling rise in the global significance of Islam, which in the context of the Horn is most sharply illustrated by the growing linkages between northeast Africa and the adjacent Arabian peninsula. Physically close to one another, and connected over many centuries by trade and cultural relations, most obviously religion, these regions have become separated in international affairs, initially as a result of European colonialism, and subsequently through conventions of diplomatic practice that turned Africa into a self-contained arena defined most obviously by the OAU and then the AU. African diplomacy was in turn concerned primarily with resolving conflicts within the continent, and secondarily with the continent's relations with the historical centres of influence represented by colonialism and the Cold War. The emergence of an active and extremely conflictual international politics of Islam threatens to disrupt these long-established assumptions. At one level, the upheavals prompted by much more activist forms of Islam, notably Salafism and the creation of organisations such as *al-Shabaab*, have had a direct impact on the Horn. At another, conflicts within the Arabian peninsula and notably the war in Yemen have provided openings for states within the Horn, enabling Eritrea for example to reduce its diplomatic isolation and gain allies and sources of cash. Djibouti has been another obvious beneficiary. Both Saudi Arabia and the Gulf states have started to play a much more active role in the region, though the virtual absence of Shia Islam has limited the influence of Iran. At a much more basic level, Islam threatens to empower the peripheries of the Horn against the centre, by providing a source of ideological inspiration allied to other and notably financial resources, and in the process reactivating a very ancient characterisation of the region in which the 'highland core' (not only in Ethiopia, but also in Eritrea), viewed throughout this book as the relatively stable centre from which power ultimately emanates, may instead be threatened by its peripheries. This is a part of the world constantly in flux, in which patterns of state creation and decay form and reform, in response to the ever changing relations between highland and lowland, Christianity and Islam, zones of settled governance and zones of statelessness. It would be foolish to assume that these tensions are being, or will ever be, resolved.

NOTES

INTRODUCTION: AN AFRICAN ANOMALY

1. de Waal, *The Real Politics of the Horn of Africa*, op. cit..

1. THE POWER OF LANDSCAPE

1. I owe this insight to James Hammond; see his website at: http://www. bbk.ac.uk/geology/our-staff/james-hammond/research-interests
2. Markakis, *Ethiopia: The Last Two Frontiers*; the first chapter of this book provides a superb synopsis of the cultural and political structure of the region that applies beyond Ethiopia to the Horn as a whole.
3. Lefort, 'Powers—*mengist*—and peasants in rural Ethiopia'.
4. Levine, *Wax & Gold*, p. 93.
5. See Fantini, 'Go Pente!'.
6. Ethiopia Census 2007, online.
7. Wikipedia, Somalis in the UK, online.
8. Wikipedia, Somali-Americans, online.
9. Wikipedia, Ethiopian-Americans, online.
10. Eritrea Population and Health Survey 2010, online.
11. UN World Population Prospects, 2010 revision, cited in Wikipedia, Demographics of Ethiopia, online. There is no indication of whether these figures include Eritrea (which was separate from Ethiopia in 1950, part of it in 1980, and separate again in 2010), though the relatively even rate of population growth suggests that Eritrea is excluded.
12. Worldometers, Ethiopia population, online.

2. HISTORIES OF STATE CREATION AND COLLAPSE

1. The text is available in Greenfield, *Ethiopia: A New Political History*, p. 464.
2. For a general history of Ethiopia, see Henze, *Layers of Time*; for modern Ethiopia, see Bahru Zewde, *A History of Modern Ethiopia*.
3. See Bahru Zewde, *The Quest for Socialist Utopia*.
4. See Skocpol, *States and Social Revolutions*.
5. The Ethiopian revolution has been extensively documented. See Andargachew Tiruneh, *The Ethiopian Revolution*; Clapham, *Transformation and Continuity*; Halliday & Molyneux, *The Ethiopian Revolution*; René Lefort, *Ethiopia*.
6. See Clapham, *Transformation and Continuity*.
7. See Pool, *From Guerrillas to Government*.
8. *The Ethiopian Herald*, 27 June 1979.
9. Connell, *Against All Odds*.
10. I am not aware of any figures, or even rough estimates, for deaths as a result of the wars in Eritrea and Tigray, but there can be little doubt that they ran at least into hundreds of thousands, and very possibly millions. One Ethiopian source, long after the event, suggests 250,000–300,000 Ethiopian dead for the war in Eritrea up to 1991 (see http://www.madote.com/2014/07/how-ethiopian-general-tsadkan-cried.html).
11. See Young, *Peasant Revolution in Ethiopia*.
12. For an account of the battle derived largely from the Ethiopian military archives, see Gebru Tareke, 'From Af Abet to Shire'.
13. See Tekeste Negash & Tronvoll, *Brothers at War*, pp.17–18.
14. See notably Laitin & Samatar, *Somalia*; and Lewis, *A Modern History of Somalia*.
15. See Yordanov, *The Soviet Union and the Horn of Africa*.
16. The two outstanding analyses of African statehood are Bayart, *The State in Africa*, and Herbst, *States and Power in Africa*. For two edited volumes on state failure, both with a particular emphasis on Africa, see Rotberg, *When States Fail*, and Zartman, *Collapsed States*.
17. See Bayart, *The State in Africa*.

3. STATE RECONSTRUCTION IN ETHIOPIA

1. This was not his original name. He was initially called Legesse (Zenawi, following Ethiopian usage, being his father's name), but took the name of Meles in order to perpetuate the memory of one of his comrades, Meles Teckle, who had been killed by the *Derg* in 1975.

2. A personal note: by far the leading secondary school in Ethiopia in the 1960s was the General Wingate School in Addis Ababa, funded by the United Kingdom with largely British staff, and named after a British army officer who had been prominent in the liberation from Italian rule. Its headmaster at that time, John Royds, established a scholarship scheme, under which students chosen on the basis of academic merit would receive free education at the school. "God knows what is going to happen to this country", he told me then, "but if we can find the brightest kids in Ethiopia, and give them the best education we can, one or other of them, sooner or later, will be able to do something." One of those scholarship boys was the future Meles Zenawi.

3. Young, 1997, p. 96.

4. See Smith 2013.

5. Ethiopia, 2005 Constitution, online.

6. See Soares de Oliveira 2011; Jones et al. 2013.

7. See Levine 1965. In the metaphor, the 'wax' refers to the visible outer form, the 'gold' to the inner reality. See also Vaughan & Tronvoll 2003.

8. Unlike every other African state of which I am aware, in which the head of government is the President, Ethiopia has a titular president, and the Prime Minister is head of government, a provision that derives from Meles Zenawi's complete lack of interest in being formal head of state.

9. See US State Department and Human Rights Watch report, online.

10. See Markakis 2011, pp. 341–51.

11. Ibid., ch.13.

12. I have seen no documented analysis of the Ethiopian reaction to the Eritrean occupation of the contested zone, and this account is derived from my own interviews and impressions at the time.

13. See Leenco Latta, 'Ethiopia: the path to war, and the consequences of peace', in Jacquin-Berdal & Plaut 2004, pp. 43–45.

14. I can find no written record of Ethiopian reactions to the Eritrean demarche, and this account is taken from my own interviews in Addis Ababa shortly afterwards. On public and intra-TPLF opinions on the issue, see Leenco Latta 2004, esp. pp. 48–50; on the revival of Ethiopian nationalism, see Tronvoll 2009, esp. ch. 6.

15. See Tronvoll 2009 for a much more detailed examination of this issue.

16. Pausewang & al. 2002, p. 230.

17. See Gilkes 2015.

18. The four leaders identified under this heading, Yoweri Museveni in Uganda (1986), Isayas Afewerki in Eritrea (1991), Meles Zenawi in Ethiopia (1991), and Paul Kagame in Rwanda (1994), had all come to power as the reforming leaders of well-organised insurgencies. Although all four were to hold power for over twenty years, the very different trajectories of the states concerned revealed flaws in the model that they were deemed to represent. See Ottaway 1999.

19. I once sceptically asked him, in the early years of the EPRDF regime, whether ADLI would actually work. With characteristic disarming frankness, he replied: "I don't know. We thought we'd give it a go. If it doesn't work, we'll try something else."

20. See de Waal 2013.

21. See Fourie 2015.

22. Technically, 'rent' is the difference between the costs of producing and distributing a good, and the amount for which it can be sold on the open market. 'Oil rents', for example, have at times amounted to a massive difference between the cost of pumping, distributing and refining petroleum products, and global oil prices determined by supply and demand, which in turn accrued principally to the oil-producing states.

23. Economic growth rates in Ethiopia have been contested. The government has been so determined to foster the mantra of 'double-digit growth' that it has been suspected of manipulating the figures so as to make them conform to its aspirations. IMF figures have generally been lower. There can however be no doubt, confirmed by observation throughout the country, that a very impressive level has been achieved.

24. Aspen, 'Rural Land and Urban Aspirations'.

25. See Relief Web, online.

26. For an overview, see Kelsall 2013, especially Chapter 4 on Ethiopia.

27. See Kamski, online.

28. According to UNCTAD, online, foreign direct investment, while varying significantly from year to year, rose from $US135m in 2000 to $953m in 2013.

29. See Kelsall 2013, pp.108–10; and Ayelech & Helmsing 2010.

30. See Kelsall 2013, pp.110–11; and Tegegne Gebre-Egziabher 2007. See also Arkebe Oqubay 2015; the author is Special Adviser on Industrial Policy in the Office of the Prime Minister in Addis Ababa, and accordingly writes from an internal perspective, but the book is both analytical and carefully researched.

31. UNDP 2014, online, p.19, Fig.2.5.

32. World Bank, Ease of Doing Business Index, online.

33. Global Entrepreneurship Index, online.

34. The only two partial cases are the succession to Menilek of his grandson Lej Iyasu in 1913, which lasted only until his overthrow in a coup d'état in 1916; and that of Negus Teferi (who then took the name of Haile Sellassie) to Empress Zauditu in 1930, at which point he was already effective head of government.

35. Author's interview with Hailemariam Desalegn.

36. See BBC, January 2016, online.

37. A classic expression of this view was the proclamation issued by the leaders of the attempted *coup d'état* against the imperial regime in December 1960, published in Greenfield 1965, pp.398–99.

4. ERITREA: THE TRAGEDY OF THE POST-INSURGENT STATE

1. I have explored the broader problems of post-liberation governance, of which Eritrea provides an extreme example, in Clapham 2012 online.

2. The Chairman of the Constitutional Commission has recorded his experiences in Bereket 2011, pp. 105–131.

3. See Tronvoll 1998.

4. Ibid.

5. See O'Kane & Hepner 2009.

6. See Styan 2004.

7. See Guazzini 2009. This is the best available history of the border, and also notes the inadequacy or duplicity of the Italian maps of the region.

8. See Plaut 2004b.

9. See Plaut 2004a; and Tekeste Negash & Tronvoll 2000.

10. See Gebru Tareke 2004.

11. See Plaut 2004b.

12. Isayas Afewerki is on record as giving a total of 19,000 Eritrean deaths (IRIN News, online), but well-informed (and necessarily anonymous) sources in Asmara suggest that the actual total was about 40,000. There are no official figures of which I am aware on the Ethiopian side, but one military source gives a total of 98,700 Ethiopians killed during the first year of the war, due to 'an extremely inept and embarrassing war plan' (Madote.com online), which would suggest a total of about 120,000 overall.

13. The outstanding work on the international legal implications of the conflict, de Guttry et al. 2009, devotes seventeen chapters (280 pp.) to issues within the remit of the Claims Commission, as against only four chapters (117 pp.) to issues concerned with the boundary.

14. Available at EEBC 2002, online.

15. The only reference to a two-year war resulting in about 160,000 deaths states appears at ibid., p.13: 'In May 1998, hostilities broke out between Eritrea and Ethiopia. After a number of attempts to re-establish peace between the two Parties, the December Agreement was signed on 12 December 2000, providing for the permanent termination of military hostilities between them.'

16. The legal implications of the Algiers accord are examined in Nystuen & Tronvoll 2008.

17. See Pool 2001, pp. 76–82.

18. See Amnesty International 2001 and subsequent reports.

19. See Plaut 2016, for a fascinating leaked appraisal of Isayas from the US ambassador in Asmara, Ronald K. McMullen. I am most grateful to the author for allowing me to access a pre-publication text.

20. See Gaim Kibreab 2009.

21. Ibid. Warsai refers to inheritors or successors (i.e. the new generation of youthful conscripts), yikaalo to the heroes of the liberation struggle.

22. See Gaim Kibreab, loc.cit. See also Commission of Inquiry 2015, online. For an appraisal of human rights in Eritrea, see Tronvoll & Mekonnen 2014.
23. UNHCR 2014, online, Table 2.
24. There are no official population figures for Eritrea, but see Eritrea Population and Health Survey 2010, online. This ranking takes the estimates from Wikipedia populations, online, accessed 06.05.2016.
25. See Dictatorships blogspot, online, accessed 09.05.2016.
26. See Müller 2009.
27. Seen Plaut, 2016, Ch.4, 'Eritrea's Economy—Smoke and Mirrors'.
28. See Nevsun, Bisha mine, online.
29. de Waal 2015, p.152.
30. See Plaut, 2016, and de Waal 2015, Ch.9.
31. See UN Security Council, online.
32. See Jones et al. 2013.
33. This finding derives from research by Gaim Kibreab, to whom I am grateful for the opportunity to consult his forthcoming book on the Eritrean National Service.
34. de Waal 2015, p.153.

5. MANAGING SOMALI STATES

1. See Clapham 1998, for a comparative survey that illustrates this point.
2. Somali names are notoriously confusing, not least as a result of the prevalence of names like Mohamed, Ahmed and Ali, and it is normal to refer to individuals by a name that is more distinctive than the others, or by a nickname. President Ahmed Mohamed Mohamed of Somaliland, for example, is generally referred to as 'Silanyo' meaning 'the lizard'. It is testimony to the egalitarian ethos of Somali society that leading figures are expected to accept such unflattering names, and would only incur derision by trying to reject them. On Somali names, see Hoehne 2010a. Somali names are often written according to the conventions developed for spelling the language in Roman script, in which redundant letters such as 'c' and 'x' are used for sounds for which there is no precise Roman equivalent, so that 'Mohamed', for example, becomes 'Maxamed', and the town of Burao becomes 'Burco'. Here, the normal Western spellings are used.

3. See de Waal 2015, p. 117.
4. Menkhaus 2003, cited in de Waal 2015, p. 118.
5. See Stremlau & Ridwan Osman 2015.
6. Ibid.
7. See Hansen 2016, p.15. The following section draws heavily on Hansen's account.
8. This evidence derives largely from the 'Wikileaks' release of classified US documents, which I have not been able to examine.
9. Transparency International, online, accessed 20 May 2016.
10. See, notably, Mills 2014.
11. See Maxwell & Nisar Majid 2016, on which this account depends.
12. See Hansen 2016 for the best account of *Al-Shabaab*.
13. See Olsen 2000.
14. See Gérard Prunier 2010, for a comparison of British and Italian colonialism in Somalia.
15. See Walls 2014, p.150 et seq. This provides the basic account of the Somaliland experience.
16. See Walls, op.cit.; Bradbury 2008; de Waal 2015, Ch. 8, for more detailed accounts of these negotiations and their outcomes.
17. See de Waal 2015, pp.134–5.
18. See Walls 2014, pp. 229–33.
19. See Hoehne 2010b; and Hoehne 2006.
20. For a much more detailed account, see Markakis 2011, Ch.13, pp. 306–28.
21. See Wikipedia, ONLF, online.
22. A nickname inherited from his father, who did indeed have one eye.
23. '*Liyu*' is simply the Amharic word for 'special', and the name applies to the paramilitary police force in each region; in the Somali region, however, it has acquired a particular significance.
24. Material on Djibouti is exceptionally sparse. For historical background, see Thompson & Adloff 1968. For recent developments, see Styan 2013.
25. 'The Superpowers' Playground', *The Economist* (London), 9 April 2016.

6. THE HORN, THE CONTINENT AND THE WORLD

1. de Waal 2015.
2. For an overview of Ethiopia's regional relations since 1991, see Medhane Tadesse 2015.
3. See Goitom Gebreluel 2014.
4. Verhoeven 2015.
5. See Kamski 2016.
6. See Wikipedia, Lamu Port, online. the website at: https://en.wikipedia. org/wiki/Lamu_Port_and_Lamu-Southern_Sudan-Ethiopia_ Transport_Corridor

BIBLIOGRAPHY

Andargachew Tiruneh, 1993. *The Ethiopian Revolution 1974–1987*, Cambridge: Cambridge U.P.

Arkebe Oqubay, 2015. *Made in Africa: Industrial Policy in Ethiopia*, Oxford: Oxford U.P.

Aspen, Harald, 'Rural Land and Urban Aspirations: Future Orientation in a Time of Change', unpublished ms.

Ayelech Tiruwha Melese & A.H.J. Helmsing, 2010. 'Endogenisation or enclave formation? The development of the Ethiopian cut flower industry', *Journal of Modern African Studies*, Vol. 48, No. 1, pp. 35–66.

Bahru Zewde, 2002. *A History of Modern Ethiopia, 1855–1991*, London: James Currey.

———, 2014. *The Quest for Socialist Utopia: The Ethiopian Student Movement, c1960–1974*, London: James Currey.

Bayart, Jean-François, 1993. *The State in Africa: The Politics of the Belly*, London: Longman.

Bereket Habte Selassie, 2011. *Wounded Nation: How a Once Promising Eritrea was Betrayed and its Future Compromised*, Trenton, NJ: Red Sea Press.

Bradbury, Mark, 2008. *Becoming Somaliland*, Oxford: James Currey.

Clapham, Christopher, ed. 1998. *African Guerrillas*, Oxford: James Currey.

———, 1990. *Transformation and Continuity in Revolutionary Ethiopia*, Cambridge: Cambridge U.P.

Connell, Dan, 1993. *Against All Odds*, Trenton, NJ: Red Sea Press.

Guazzini, Federica, 2009. 'The Eritrean-Ethiopian boundary conflict: the physical border and the human border', in de Guttry et al. eds., pp.109–139.

de Guttry, Andrea, Harry H.G. Post & Gabriella Venturini, eds., 2009. *The 1998–2000 War Between Eritrea and Ethiopia: An International Legal Perspective*, The Hague: T.M.C. Asser Press.

Dereje Feyissa & Markus Hoehne, eds., 2010. *Borders & Borderlands as Resources in the Horn of Africa*, Woodbridge: James Currey.

de Waal, Alex, 2013. 'The theory and practice of Meles Zenawi', *African Affairs*, Vol.112, No. 446, pp. 148–55.

———, 2015. *The Real Politics of the Horn of Africa: Money, War and the Business of Power*, London: Polity Press.

Fantini, Emanuele, 2015, 'Go Pente! The Charismatic Renewal of the Evangelical Movement in Ethiopia', in Prunier & Ficquet, eds., 2015, pp.123–46.

Fourie, Elsje, 2015. 'China's example for Meles' Ethiopia: when development "models" land', *Journal of Modern African Studies*, Vol. 53, No. 3, pp. 289–316.

Gaim Kibreab, 2009. 'Forced Labour in Eritrea', *The Journal of Modern African Studies*, Vol. 47 No.1, pp. 41–72.

———, forthcoming. *The Eritrean National Service: Servitude for the "Common Good" & the Youth Exodus*.

Gebru Tareke, 2004. 'From Af Abet to Shire: the Defeat and Demise of Ethiopia's "Red" Army, 1988–89', *The Journal of Modern African Studies*, Vol. 42, No. 2, pp. 239–281.

Gilkes, Patrick, 2015. 'Elections and Politics in Ethiopia, 2005–2010', in Prunier & Ficquet, eds. pp. 313–331.

Goitom Gebreluel, 2014. 'Ethiopia's Grand Renaissance Dam: Ending Africa's Oldest Geopolitical Rivalry?', *The Washington Quarterly*, Vol. 37, No. 2, pp. 25–37.

Greenfield, Richard, 1965 *Ethiopia: A New Political History*, London: Pall Mall Press.

Halliday Fred, & Maxine Molyneux, 1981. *The Ethiopian Revolution*, London: Verso.

Hansen, Stig Jarle, 2016. *Al-Shabaab in Somalia: The History and Ideology of a Militant Islamist Group*, London: Hurst, revised edn.

BIBLIOGRAPHY

Henze, Paul, 2000. *Layers of Time: A History of Ethiopia*, London: Hurst.

Herbst, Jeffrey, 2000. *States and Power in Africa: Comparative Lessons in Authority and Control*, Princeton, NJ: Princeton University Press.

Hoehne, Markus, 2006. 'Political identity, emerging state structures and conflict in northern Somalia', *Journal of Modern African Studies*, Vol. 46, No. 3, pp. 397–414.

Hoehne, Markus & Virginia Luling, eds., 2010. *Milk and Peace, Drought and War: Somali Culture, Society and Politics*, London: Hurst.

———, 2010a, 'Somali (nick)names and their meanings', in Hoehne & Luling, eds., 2010, pp. 345–363.

———, 2010b, 'People & Politics along & across the Somaliland-Puntland Border', in Dereje Feyissa & Hoehne 2010, pp. 97–121

Jacquin-Berdal, Dominique & Martin Plaut, eds., 2004. *Unfinished Business: Ethiopia and Eritrea at War*, Trenton, NJ: Red Sea Press.

Jones, Will, Ricardo Soares de Oliveira & Harry Verhoeven, 2013, *Africa's Illiberal State-Builders*, Oxford University Refugee Studies Centre, Working Paper No. 89, online at https://www.rsc.ox.ac.uk/files/publications/working-paper-series/wp89-africas-illiberal-state-builders-2013.pdf

Kamski, Benedikt, 2016. 'The Kuraz Sugar Development Project', Briefing Note 1, Omo-Turkana Basin Research Network.

Kelsall, Tim, 2013. *Business, Politics and the State in Africa: Challenging the Orthodoxies on Growth and Transformation*, London: Zed Books.

Laitin, David D. & Said Sheikh Samatar, 1987. *Somalia: Nation in Search of a State*, Boulder, CO: Westview.

Leenco Latta, 2004. 'Ethiopia: the path to war and the consequences of peace', in Jacquin-Berdal & Plaut, eds., pp. 37–56.

Lefort, René, 1981. *Ethiopia: An Heretical Revolution?*, London: Zed.

———, 2010. 'Powers—*mengist*—and peasants in rural Ethiopia: the post-2005 interlude', *Journal of Modern African Studies*, Vol. 48, No. 3, pp. 435–60.

Levine, Donald N., 1965. *Wax & Gold: Tradition and Innovation in Ethiopian Culture*, Chicago, IL: University of Chicago Press.

Lewis, Ioan M., 1980. *A Modern History of Somalia*, London: Longman.

Markakis, John, 2011. *Ethiopia: The Last Two Frontiers*, Woodbridge: James Currey.

BIBLIOGRAPHY

Maxwell, Daniel, & Nisar Majid, 2016. *Famine in Somalia: Competing Imperatives, Collective Failures, 2011–12*, London: Hurst.

Medhane Tadesse, 2015. 'Making Sense of Ethiopia's Regional Influence', in Prunier & Ficquet, eds., pp. 333–56.

Menkhaus, Ken, 2003. 'State Collapse in Somalia: Second Thoughts', *Review of African Political Economy*, 30, pp. 405–22.

Mills, Greg, 2014. *Why States Recover: Changing Walking Societies into Winning Nations—from Afghanistan to Zimbabwe*, London: Hurst.

Müller, Tanja R. 2009. 'Human Resource Development and the State: Higher Education in Postrevolutionary Eritrea', in O'Kane & Hepner, eds., Ch. 4.

Nystuen, Gro & Kjetil Tronvoll, 2008. 'The Eritrea-Ethiopian Peace Agreement: Exploring the Limits of Law', *Nordic Journal of Human Rights*, Vol. 26, No.1, pp.16–37.

O'Kane, David & Tricia Redeker Hepner, eds., 2009. *Biopolitics, Militarism and Development: Eritrea in the Twenty-First Century*, New York: Berghahn.

Olson, Mancur, 2000. *Power and Prosperity: Outgrowing Communist and Capitalist Dictatorships*, New York: Basic Books.

Ottaway, Marina, 1999. *Africa's New Leaders: Democracy or State Reconstruction?* Washington, DC: Carnegie Endowment.

Pausewang, Siegfried, Kjetil Tronvoll & Lovise Aalen, eds., 2002. *Ethiopia since the Derg: A Decade of Democratic Pretension and Performance*, London: Zed Books.

Plaut, Martin, 2004a, 'Background to war: from friends to foes', in Jacquin-Berdal & Plaut, pp.1–22.

———, 2004b. 'The conflict and its aftermath', in Jacquin-Berdal & Plaut, eds., pp. 87–123.

———, 2016, *Understanding Eritrea: Inside Africa's Most Repressive State*, London: Hurst.

Pool, David, 2001. *From Guerrillas to Government: The Eritrean People's Liberation Front*, Oxford: James Currey.

Prunier, Gérard, 2010, 'Benign Neglect versus *La Grande Somalia*: the Colonial Legacy and the Post-Colonial Somali State', in Hoehne & Luling, eds., pp.35–49

BIBLIOGRAPHY

Prunier, Gérard & Eloi Ficquet, eds., 2015. *Understanding Contemporary Ethiopia: Monarchy, Revolution and the Legacy of Meles Zenawi*, London: Hurst.

Rotberg, Robert I., ed. 2004. *When States Fail: Causes and Consequences*, Princeton, NJ: Princeton U.P.

Skocpol, Theda, 1979. *States and Social Revolutions*, Cambridge: Cambridge U.P.

Smith, Lahra, 2013. *Making Citizens in Africa: Ethnicity, Gender and National Identity in Ethiopia*, Cambridge, Cambridge U.P. 2013.

Soares de Oliveira, Ricardo, 2011. 'Illiberal Peacebuilding in Angola', *Journal of Modern African Studies*, Vol. 49, No. 2, pp. 287–314.

Stremlau, Nicole & Ridwan Osman, 2015. 'Courts, Clans and Companies: Mobile Money and Dispute Resolution in Somaliland', *Stability: Journal of International Development*, Vol. 4, No.1, pp.1–15.

Styan, David, 2004. 'Twisting Ethio-Eritrean economic ties: misperceptions of war and the misplaced priorities of peace, 1997–2002', in Jacquin-Berdal & Plaut, eds., pp.201–228.

———, 'Djibouti: Changing Influence in the Horn's Strategic Hub', London: RIIA, 2013.

Tegegne Gebre-Egziabher, 2007. 'Impacts of Chinese imports and coping strategies of local producers: the case of small scale footwear enterprises in Ethiopia', *Journal of Modern African Studies*, Vol. 45, No. 4, pp. 647–79.

Tekeste Negash & Kjetil Tronvoll, 2000. *Brothers at War: Making Sense of the Eritrean-Ethiopian War*, Oxford: James Currey.

Thompson, Virginia & Richard Adloff, 1968, *Djibouti and the Horn of Africa*, Stanford, CA: Stanford U.P.

Tronvoll, Kjetil, 1998. 'The process of nation-building in post-war Eritrea: created from below or directed from above?', *The Journal of Modern African Studies*, Vol. 36, No. 3, pp. 461–82.

———, 2009. *War & the Politics of Identity in Ethiopia: the making of enemies and allies in the Horn of Africa*, Woodbridge, James Currey.

——— & Daniel R. Mekonnen, 2014. *The African Garrison State: Human Rights and Political Development in Eritrea*, Woodbridge: James Currey.

Vaughan, Sarah & Kjetil Tronvoll, 2003. *The Culture of Power in Contemporary Ethiopian Political Life*, Stockholm, SIDA Studies No.10.

BIBLIOGRAPHY

Verhoeven, Harry, 2015. *Water, Civilisation and Power in Sudan: The Political Economy of Military-Islamist Statebuilding*, Cambridge: Cambridge U.P.

Walls, Michael, 2014. *A Somali Nation-State: History, Culture and Somaliland's Political Transition*, Pisa: Ponte Invisibile.

Yordanov, Radoslav A., 2016. *The Soviet Union and the Horn of Africa during the Cold War*, London: Lexington Books.

Young, John, 1997. *Peasant Revolution in Ethiopia: The Tigray People's Liberation Front, 1975–1991*, Cambridge: Cambridge U.P.

Zartman, I. William, 1995. *Collapsed States: The Disintegration and Restoration of Legitimate Authority*, Boulder, CO: Lynne Rienner.

Online Sources

Amnesty International, 2001: https://www.amnesty.org/en/documents/afr64/002/2001/en/

British Broadcasting Corporation, January 2016: http://www.bbc.co.uk/news/world-africa-35325536

Countrymeters: http://countrymeters.info/en/

Clapham, Christopher, 2012: 'From Liberation Movement to Government: Past legacies and the challenge of transition in Africa', Brenthurst Discussion Paper 8/2012, The Brenthurst Foundation, Johannesburg: http://www.thebrenthurstfoundation.org/files/Brenthurst_Commisioned_Reports/Brenthurst-paper-201208-From-Liberation-Movement-to-Government.pdf

Commission of Inquiry on Human Rights in Eritrea, 2015: http://www.ohchr.org/EN/HRBodies/HRC/CoIEritrea

Dictatorships blogspot: http://dictatorshipsandfailedstates.blogspot.co.uk/2014/12/eritrea-oppression-refugees-and-dissent.html

Eritrea Population and Health Survey 2010: NSO-2013_Eritrea-household-polulation-survey%20(1).pdf

Ethiopia Census 2007, population figures by ethnic group: http://www.csa.gov.et/newcsaweb/images/documents/surveys/Population%20and%20Housing%20census/ETH-pop-2007/survey0/data/Doc/Reports/National_Statistical.pdf

Ethiopia, Constitution of the Federal Democratic Republic of Ethiopia, 2005:: http://www.wipo.int/edocs/lexdocs/laws/en/et/et007en.pdf

BIBLIOGRAPHY

Ethiopia-Eritrea Boundary Commission Report 2002: http://www.peaceau.org/uploads/ethiopia-eritrea-decision-13–04–2002.pdf.

Global Entrepreneurship Index: https://thegedi.org/global-entrepreneurship-and-development-index/

Human Rights Watch, Report: https://www.hrw.org/legacy/wr2k3/africa5.html.

IRIN News: http://www.irinnews.org/report/22303/eritrea-president-says-19000-killed-border-war

Kamski, Benedikt, 'The Kuraz Sugar Development Project', Omo-Turkana Basin Research Network, Briefing Note No.1, June 2016: file://ksdp_briefing_note_omo_turkana_basin_research_network_1.pdf

Madote.com: http://www.madote.com/2014/07/how-ethiopian-general-tsadkan-cried.html

Relief Web: http://reliefweb.int/report/ethiopia/ethiopia-millennium-development-goals-report-2014-assessment-ethiopia-s-progress.

Nevsun, Bisha mine: http://www.nevsun.com/projects/bisha-main/

Transparency International, Corruption Perceptions Index 2015: http://www.transparency.org/cpi2015?gclid=CNO7ycKe6MwCFcyRGwod-SUECA

UNCTAD, foreign direct investment figures: http://unctadstat.unctad.org/wds/TableViewer/tableView.aspx

UNDP, *National Human Development Report Ethiopia 2014*: http://www.et.undp.org/content/dam/ethiopia/docs/ENDHR_Accelerating%20Inclusive%20Growth%20for%20%20Sustainable%20Human%20Development%20in%20Ethiopia_finalweb.pdf.

UNHCR 2014: http://www.unhcr.org/56655f4b3.html.

UN Security Council: https://www.un.org/sc/suborg/en/sanctions/751

US State Department, Human Rights Report 2002: http://www.state.gov/j/drl/rls/hrrpt/2002/18203.htm

Wikipedia, Demographics of Ethiopia: https://en.wikipedia.org/wiki/Demographics_of_Ethiopia

Wikipedia, Ethiopian-Americans: https://en.wikipedia.org/wiki/Ethiopian_Americans Wikipedia, Lamu Port: https://en.wikipedia.org/wiki/Lamu_ort_and_Lamu-Southern_Sudan-Ethiopia_Transport_Corridor

Wikipedia, ONLF: https://en.wikipedia.org/wiki/Ogaden_National_Liberation_Front.

BIBLIOGRAPHY

Wikipedia, Somalis in the UK: https://en.wikipedia.org/wiki/Somalis_
in_the_United_Kingdom#Naturalisation_and_grants_of_settlement

Wikipedia, populations: https:// en.wikipedia.org/wiki/List_of_countries_
of_countries_and_dependencies_by_population

Wikipedia, Somali-Americans: https://en.wikipedia.org/wiki/Somali_
Americans

World Bank, *Ease of Doing Business Index*: www.doingbusiness.org

Worldometers, Ethiopia population: http://www.worldometers.info/
world-population/ethiopia-population/

INDEX

INDEX

INDEX

INDEX

Nationalities and People's Regional State (SNNPRS), 25, 74; Southern Region, 87, 89–90, 102–3, 107; strikes (1974), 43; Tigray, 66–7, 83, 106, 121; Welega, 100; Welo, 23, 43, 96; Zalambesa, 127

Ethiopian Air Lines: 40

Ethiopian People's Democratic Movement (EPDM): as ANDM, 71–2

Ethiopian People's Revolutionary Democratic Front (EPRDF): 53, 69–71, 74–5, 77–80, 89, 94, 99, 102, 105, 108, 113, 118, 168–9, 190; accession of (1991), 12, 51, 110–11, 188; coalition-building strategy of, 103; electoral performance of (2005), 89–90; electoral performance of (2015), 91; formation of, 68; members of, 79, 82, 87, 90; Oromo People's Democratic Organisation (OPDO), 72; Transitional Charter, 70

Ethiopian People's Revolutionary Party (EPRP): 44

Ethiopian Somali Democratic League (ESDL): 169

Ethiopian Sugar Corporation: 99

ethnic cleansing: 27

European Union (EU): 135, 190

fascism: 180; Italian, 35, 40

federalism: ethnically-based, 27, 71, 76, 105–6

Federation of Ethiopia and Eritrea (1952–62): 38–9; international focus on, 188–9

feudalism: 56

Finland: 102

First Italo-Ethiopian War (1894–6): Battle of Adwa (1896), 31

First World War (1914–18): 123

France: 59; Revolution (1789–99), 43, 45, 179

French Somali Coast (1896–1967): 3, 53, 142, 170; as French Territory of the Afars and Issas, 59, 170; creation of, 36; referendum (1958), 59; referendum (1967), 59

French Territory of the Afars and Issas (1967–77): 59, 170

Front for the Restoration of Unity and Democracy (FRUD): 173

gada: concept of, 23

Gadabursi (clan/Dir sub-clan): 164; territory inhabited by, 58, 161

Gamu (ethnic group): 74

de Gaulle, Charles: 59

Germany: 37

al-Ghazi, Imam Ahmad ibn Ibrahim (Ahmed Gragn): 15–16

Gibe, River: 96

Global Entrepreneurship Index (2016): 101

Gofa (ethnic group): 74

INDEX

INDEX

INDEX

INDEX

INDEX

INDEX

28; Hoover Dam, 185; military of, 174; Somali population of, 28

Vietnam War (1955–75): political impact of, 46

de Waal, Alex: 4, 140, 181
Wabi Shabele: valley of, 14, 18
War on Terror: 154
Warsai-Yikaalo Development Campaign (WYDC): launch of (2002), 131
Warsangeli (Darood sub-clan): territory inhabited by, 161, 166
Washington Consensus: 97, 189
Welayta (ethnic group): 74, 78, 81; as member of SNNPR, 25
Western Somali Liberation Front: role in Ogaden War (1977–8), 57

White Nile: 32
World Bank: *Ease of Doing Business Index*, 101; 'food-for-work' programme, 98
Worldometers: 30
Workers' Party of Ethiopia: inauguration of (1984), 46–7

xeer: 149–50; concept of, 20–1

Yeha: 11
Yemen: 121, 151; Aden, 37; Christian population of, 140; Civil War (2015), 134, 140, 174; Muslim population of, 140

Zambezi, River: 185; Cahora Bassa Dam, 185; Kariba Dam, 185
Zimbabwe: 53